INCREDIBLE
IDEAS for Youth Groups

OTHER YOUTH SPECIALTIES BOOKS

Called to Care
Creative Socials and Special Events
Far-Out Ideas for Youth Groups
Good Clean Fun
Great Ideas for Small Youth Groups
Greatest Skits on Earth
Greatest Skits on Earth, Volume 2
High School Ministry
High School TalkSheets
Holiday Ideas for Youth Groups
Hot Talks
Ideas for Social Action
Incredible Ideas for Youth Groups
Intensive Care
Junior High Ministry
Junior High TalkSheets
Organizing Your Youth Ministry
Play It! Great Games for Groups
Super Ideas for Youth Groups
Tension Getters
Tension Getters II
Unsung Heroes
Way-Out Ideas for Youth Groups
Youth Specialties Clip Art Book
Youth Specialties Clip Art Book, Volume Two

INCREDIBLE IDEAS for Youth Groups

Wayne Rice & Mike Yaconelli

Youth Specialties

ZONDERVAN PUBLISHING HOUSE
Grand Rapids, Michigan

Zondervan Publishing House, 1415 Lake Drive, S.E., Grand Rapids, Michigan 49506

Library of Congress Cataloging in Publication Data
Rice, Wayne.
   Incredible ideas for youth groups.
    1. Games. 2. Amusements. 3. Youth—Recreation. I. Yaconelli, Mike. II. Title.
GV1201.R443 1982   794   82-8634
ISBN 0-310-45231-7   AACR2

Edited by Linda DeVries
Illustrations by Martha Bentley

Printed in the United States of America

88 89 90 91 92 93 94 95 / AK / 17 16 15 14 13 12 11 10

to

the youth workers

whose creativity made this book possible

Contents

Preface 9

Games 13

Crowd Breakers 47

Creative Communication 57

Skits 95

Case Studies 115

Special Events 127

Service Projects 143

Fund-raisers 149

The Family 155

Preface

Everyone likes getting together in a group. After all, groups can have fun—and fellowship—together. This book is to help you in making those times of getting together, particularly with young people, as special as possible.

Inside are hundreds of ideas that you can use for youth meetings, parties, socials, special programs, Sunday school classes, church services—most anytime at all. And they can be used with children and adults as well as with young people.

We hope you keep in mind that an idea is just that—an *idea*. There's no law that says you can't change it or adapt it or even combine it with another idea. That's called being creative, and we hope this book makes you *very* creative.

Many of the ideas in this book have already appeared in print in the *Idea* books published by Youth Specialties. We thank the many creative youth workers whose ideas appear here.

Games

Games

BACK-TO-BACK RELAY

This game may be played indoors or out. Divide the group into teams of six or more each and have the members of each team pair up. The first twosome from each team stands behind the starting line. A ball (basketball or volleyball) is placed between them just above the belt line as they stand back to back. The object of the relay is—with their arms folded in front of them and not using their elbow___ ___o carry the ball around a chair (about thirty feet away) and back again without ___ropping i___ If the ball is dropped, they must start over. When this pair successful___ ___y complete ___ir round trip, the next twosome places the ball between their backs ___ ___d does the same thing. The first team to have all of its pairs successfully comple___ ___ the relay is the winner. If a team does not have an even number, someone can ___ ___ befor. The twosomes do not need to be of the opposite sex.

This is more difficult than it may sound. The pairs must communicate and wor___ together or they will drop the ball and have to start over again and again. If they cannot do it after several attempts, have them go to the back of the line so that the rest will have a chance to try.

BASEBALL WITH STRINGS ATTACHED

Here's a variation of softball that allows a mixed group to have a competitive game. With a regular softball, some people have a hard time hitting the ball out of the infield and thus are branded "easy outs." So instead of using a softball and bat, use a tennis ball and tennis racket. Anyone can hit a good shot, and it's almost impossible to strike out. (If someone hits it too far with the new equipment, make him use either a racquetball racket or a regular bat.) This game is especially good for larger groups—with fifteen or more people on a side.

BASKETBALL SQUAT

Divide your group into teams (approximately six to ten per team). Have the teams choose a captain for each group. Then have the teams form a straight line facing the captains (approximately five to ten feet away from the captain). The captain throws the ball to the first person in the line who returns the throw and then squats down. The captain then throws the ball to the second person who does the same thing, and on down the line to the last person. The captain then throws the ball a second time to the last person, who throws it back and stands up. This process is repeated until everyone has received another pass the ball working its way up to the first person in line. Any time the ball is dropped, the team must start over again. The first team to have everybody standing up again is the winner.

BIG MOUTH STACK

Here's a game that's great for both individual competition and team relays. The object of the game is to see how high individuals or teams can stack regular alphabet blocks. The only catch is that contestants cannot use anything except their mouths to place the blocks on top of each other.

BIRTHDAY BARNYARD

This game works best with a large group. Give each person a list like the one below. After everyone has received the list, each person is instructed to look at the action described for the month of his/her birthday. When the lights are turned out, everyone is to stand up and do the appropriate action. As soon as anyone finds a person doing the same thing, they lock arms and look for the rest of their team. As soon as all of one team is together they must sit down. The first team to find all its members wins.

> January: Shout, "Happy New Year!"
> February: Say, "Be My Valentine."
> March: Blow (like the wind).
> April: Hop (to represent the Easter bunny).
> May: Say, "Mother, may I?"
> June: Say, "Will you marry me?"
> July: Make fireworks sounds.
> August: Sing, "Take me out to the ball game."
> September: Fall down.
> October: Shout, "Boo!"
> November: Say, "Gobble-gobble."
> December: Say, "Ho Ho Ho, Merry Christmas" in your best Santa Claus voice.

BLIND BALLOON HUNT

Begin by placing a number of balloons in random locations on a large floor or field (if on a field, the balloons may need to be anchored). A person is selected from each team to be a hunter. Two additional people from each team are selected to be the "guides". Blindfold the hunters. At the whistle the hunters proceed to locate as many balloons as possible (all teams going at the same time). The guides may not touch the hunters or the balloons. Allow as much time as you feel necessary. The object is for the hunters to locate as many balloons as possible and bring them back to the starting point to count. Keeping them informed of time is important in this event.

14

BLOW CUP RELAY

Give each team a fifteen-foot piece of string with a sliding paper cup on the string (see illustration).

The string is held taut and the paper cup is placed at one end. The team lines up single file. At the signal, each player must blow the cup to the other end (with hands behind his/her back) and then push it back to the start for the next player. The first team to finish wins.

BROOM WHIRL RELAY

All teams line up in straight lines and the first person of each team is given a broom. The first and second persons hold on to the broom with both hands. On signal the pair must turn around in place, so that they begin face to face, then go side to side, back to back, side to side, then face to face again. Both individuals must hold on to the broom at all times. Then the second and third persons repeat what the first and second persons did, and so on until the broom reaches the last person. That person must then run to the front of the line, with the broom, and repeat the process with the first person. The team to do this first wins. One variation is to have each pair turn around ten times before going to the next person.

BUBBLE BLOW BLITZ

Give each team a bottle of bubble soap and a bubble pipe. Have the team captain stand ten to twenty feet away from the goal line making bubbles while his teammates blow them across the goal line. The team that blows the most bubbles across the goal line wins. If you play this indoors, draw the goal line only ten feet away from the person blowing the bubbles. Dead air doesn't allow the bubbles to be blown more than a few feet. When playing outdoors the goal line can be fifteen to twenty feet away from the captain. This game does not work on windy days.

CASSETTE GAMES

Here are some ways to use a cassette tape recorder as a game resource:

1. *Name That Ad:* Record current television commercials on a cassette tape. Do not allow the name of the product to be mentioned on your tape. Then the first person in your group to name the product being advertised scores.
2. *Name That Star:* Same as above, except record the voices of current television or movie stars. Score one point for the name of the star and one point for the name of the show or movie.
3. *Name That Sound:* Record on a cassette tape various sounds from a sound effects record. (Special effects records may be borrowed from a public library.)
4. *Name That Tune:* Record current popular songs on a cassette tape while playing them at a speed which is either too fast of too slow. Score one point for the song title and one point for the recording artist.
5. *Name That Oldie:* Same as above except that in some cases it is unnecessary to vary the speed at which the recording is played.
6. *Name That Noise:* Use all the above ideas in one tape. This tape is a greater challenge because the players are caught off-guard.
7. *Miscellaneous Noises:* Other topics that could be used are: theme songs from TV shows or movies; voices of people, including children, from your church; voices of schoolteachers or disc jockeys; voices of people in your youth group; the opening lines of Bible stories, Aesop's fables, children's stories, children's songs, and hymns.

CHOP FOOEY

Provide chopsticks for each team and then race to see which team finishes eating first using only the chopsticks. The food can be anything from jello to corn.

CHRISTMAS SANTA CONTEST

Select three boys to sit in chairs and three girls to kneel in front of them. Blindfold the girls and give each of them a can of shaving cream. The object is for each girl to use the shaving cream to create a beard that resembles Santa Claus. The couple with the best-looking Santa wins.

CLOTHES ENCOUNTERS

Don't do this in an area where there is high risk of fire. In an open area in the winter this game is a lot of fun. Your group can spend a whole evening making their own UFOs and launching them. Here's how it works: These UFOs are basically hot-air ballons made out of dry-cleaning bags (usually available for a few cents each at any dry cleaning establishment), a few birthday candles, four plastic straws, and some scotch tape. Insert one end of straw No. 1 into the end of straw No. 2.

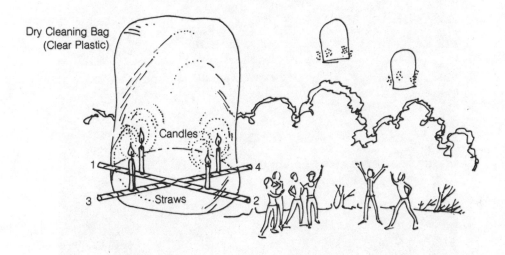

Then insert an end of straw No. 3 into the end of straw No. 4. This gives you two double-length straws. With a bit of tape, fasten the middles of the two double-length straws together to form an X. With scissors or a razor blade, make a three-inch slit along the top of each of the four straws, midway from either end.

In each slit, set four birthday candles (small ones are best). Then while someone else holds the dry-cleaning bag open-end down, poke the straws through the sides of the bag and secure them with a bit of tape. The candles should be standing up vertically inside the bag. While a couple of people hold the bag up and keep it from collapsing into the candles, light all the candles. In a few seconds, the bag will slowly fill with hot air and rise into the sky. It's quite a sight!

CLOTHESPIN HOPPING RELAY

Divide the group into at least two relay teams. The object of this game is for each player to hop in a burlap or cloth bag up to a clothesline that is full of clothespins, jump-up and grab a clothespin with his teeth, and then hop back to his team. The first team to have each member complete this task is the winner. Each team should have no more than six members, otherwise this will get boring for those awaiting their turns.

COIN, BOOK, & BALL RELAY

This relay is hilarious to watch. Divide the group into teams. Each team is given a quarter, a tennis ball (or any kind of ball that size), and a book. The idea of the relay is to balance the book on your head, hold the quarter in your eye, and place the ball between your knees, then walk to the finish line. No hands are to be used to help in any way. It's not as easy as it sounds, and it makes people look very awkward.

COOTIE

Here's a fast-moving game that accomplishes a lot. Not only do the kids have a great time, but they end up meeting and having fun with almost everyone in their youth group by the time the game is over.

Set up a number of card tables and place on each table one pair of dice, a good supply of score sheets (see example), and four pencils. Before everyone arrives, arrange the tables in a large circle or pattern that will allow movement from a lower-numbered table to the next higher-numbered table. The tables should be numbered consecutively with the No. 1 table considered the highest-numbered table. When the group arrives, make sure all the tables are full and remove any extras. Give each person a score sheet and have him write his name on the upper right-hand corner of the sheet.

	Number on Dice	Points	
	1 — Head	= 1	
	2 — Body	= 2	
	3 — Eyes	= 6	
	4 — Ears	= 8	
	5 — Tail	= 5	
	6 — Legs	= 36	

The game is ten rounds long. At the beginning of each round the people sitting across from each other are automatically partners for that round. The partners then trade score sheets at the beginning of each round to "draw the cootie" for the other while he or she rolls the dice.

Every table begins the game at the same time. Each person takes a turn rolling the die as rapidly as possible. Each number on the die corresponds to a part of the cootie's body (see score sheet). A "2" must be rolled before any other part of the body can be drawn. If a person rolls a number he can use, he keeps rolling until he rolls a number he can't use. Then he passes the die to the next person. When one person has rolled all the numbers needed to finish his cootie, he may use his turn to roll for his partner. When both partners have completed their cooties, they shout, "Cootie," and the round is over. Play stops at all tables, regardless of how far along everyone else is.

All partners then trade score sheets and have sixty seconds to add up their score and move to a new table, if necessary. Movement between rounds is as follows: The people with the highest score at each table move to the next higher numbered table (e.g., from No. 4 to No. 3). People with the lower scores at each table remain at that table. (Exception: The winners at the No. 1 table remain, while the losers at the No. 1 table move to the last table.) No one can play with the partner he or she had in the previous round. The "Great Cootie" (the winner) is the person with the highest total score for all ten rounds.

CRAZY SOCCER

To add a little excitement to an ordinary game of soccer, try this adaptation. You use the basic soccer field, only with four goals instead of two (see diagram), and you divide into four teams instead of two. Team A plays against Team C while Team B plays Team D. Each pair of teams use their own ball and are only allowed to kick their own ball.

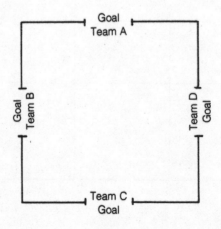

For even more variety you may combine teams so that Teams A and C play Teams B and D. One team will defend A and C goals while the other team defends B and D goals. You may use one or two balls.

Another variation would be to use the basic two-goal soccer field with a game between guys and girls—the guys have to have their legs tied with rope two and one-half feet long.

DAVID AND GOLIATH SLING THROW

Divide the group into two teams ("David I" and "David II"), with the same number of guys and girls on each team. Each team is given one old nylon stocking and one whiffle ball to place in the toe of the nylon. One person of the same sex from each team steps forward to the throwing line. Each twirls the nylon with the ball in it over his head or at his side and sees who can throw it the farthest. The winner gets one point for his or her team. The team with the most points wins the contest. You can then repeat this contest for accuracy. Set a "Goliath" (a person, chair, or other object) approximately thirty feet away from the throwing line. The person who comes the closest to "Goliath" gets one point for his or her team. If he or she should hit "Goliath," an additional bonus point is awarded to the team. The kids will quickly find out that it took much practice for David to be such a skilled marksman.

Caution: Be sure that the teams are at least ten yards to the sides of the throwing line because the slings can go forward, backward, or straight up with amateurs throwing.

√ FICTITIOUS

Here's a team game that can be lots of fun. Divide into teams of four. Write a word on the blackboard that no one has ever heard of. Give one team the actual definition and have them make up three phony definitions, then write down all four definitions. The other teams try to guess which definition is correct. Two points are given for a correct first vote and one point for a correct second vote. Each team gets a chance to write its phony definitions for a new word. The team with the most points wins.

FRISBEE RUGBY

Divide your group into two teams (this is played best with twenty-five or fewer players). Set up goals at opposite ends of the field. Team A tries to advance the frisbee over one goal line, while Team B tries to advance the frisbee over the opposite goal line. A frisbee can be advanced only by throwing it to a teammate. Each person can only take three steps before throwing the frisbee. If he takes more than three steps, the frisbee goes to the opposite team. A person must be allowed five seconds to throw the frisbee without harrassment; if he waits longer, he may be "blitzed" by his opponents. If the frisbee is dropped, or if it hits the ground before being caught, the team that had possession last must give it over to the opposing team.

FRISBEE TOURNAMENT

Here's a game that can involve your youth group for an entire afternoon or evening. Encourage everyone to bring his or her own frisbee. Bring extras for those who forget and make sure each frisbee is properly identified. Hold the event in a large open area and allow the participants to warm up before the event begins.

Singles Competition

1. *Accuracy*—Using a garden hose or rope placed on the ground, make a semicircle around an object, such as a garbage can, at which each participant will throw. Place the object about fifteen feet from all points on the semicircle. All of the competitiors throw their frisbees at the same time. Each person gets two throws at each distance. Those who hit the object from that distance remain in the game; those who miss it after two attempts are out. The object is then moved back three feet and each person left in the competition again gets two chances to hit it once. (If the group is small they may throw individually rather than at the same time.)

2. *Accuracy Opposite-handed*—The same rules apply as given above except that each person throws with his/her left hand if he/she is right-handed and vice versa.

3. *Distance*—Each person throws against those of the same age and sex. Stretch out your hose (or rope) to form straight line. From behind the line all throw at the same time unless the group is small. A judge will determine whose frisbee went the greatest distance when it came to rest (the roll is included).

4. *Distance Opposite-handed*—The same rules apply as given above, except that each person throws with his left hand if he is right-handed and vice versa.

5. *Boomerang*—Everyone competes together in this event. Have all the competitors line up in a straight line behind the marker, facing into the wind. At the signal everyone throws his frisbee at least fifteen feet into the air at an angle so that it will come back in a boomerang fashion. The person who throws the frisbee that returns closest to the throwing line is the winner.

Doubles Competition

1. *Single Frisbee Catch*—Have each participant pick a partner with whom he can compete. Two markers are stretched parallel to each other about fifteen feet apart. One partner stands behind one marker and the other partner stands behind the other marker directly opposite him. Only one frisbee is needed for each pair. Have all the frisbees on one side. At the signal all of those on one side throw their frisbees to their partners on the other side who must catch it without crossing the marker. Those who do not catch it leave the game with their partners. After each throw one marker is moved back about three feet.

2. *Opposite-handed Single Frisbee Catch*—The same rules apply as given above, except that each person throws with his left hand if he is right-handed and vice versa.

3. *Double Frisbee Catch*—Keep the same partners. Again make two parallel lines but stand about ten feet apart. The rules are the same as the "single frisbee catch" except that each person throws his frisbee at the same time and each partner must catch the other's frisbee. Emphasize that *all* frisbees are to be thrown at the same time when the signal is given.

4. *Opposite-handed Double Frisbee Catch*—The same rules apply as given above, except that each person throws with his opposite hand.

5. *Doubles' Distance*—One partner from each pair lines up at a starting point. Each throws the frisbee as far as possible in a straight line away from the starting point. Then his partner stands where the frisbee landed and at the signal throws the frisbee as far as possible. The pair with the greatest combined distance is the winner.

Team Competition

1. *Frisbee Relay*—Divide the group into teams of five to ten each. The team members form a straight line with approximately ten to fifteen yards between each member. The object is for the first person on each team to throw the frisbee to the second person and on down the line—then back to the beginning. However, the team members *cannot* move to catch it. One foot must be stationary at all times. If the frisbee cannot be caught without moving both feet, then the team member who threw it must retrieve it and throw it again from his original position. (A frisbee may be started from each end to make the event more difficult.)

2. *Opposite-handed Frisbee Relay*—The same rules apply as given above, except that each person throws with his opposite hand.

HA HA HA GAME

This is a crazy game which is good for a lot of laughs (literally). One person lies down on the floor (on his or her back), and the next person lies down with his or her head on the first person's stomach, and the next person lies down with his or her head on the second person's stomach, and so on.

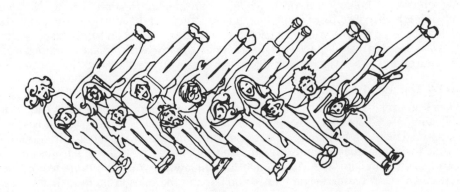

After everyone is down on the floor, the first person says, "Ha," the second says, "Ha Ha," and the third says, "Ha Ha Ha," and so on with each person adding another "Ha." It is to be done seriously, and if anyone goofs by giggling or missing the correct number of "Ha's," the group must start over. It's hilarious.

HANGER RELAY

This is a relay game for two or more teams. You will need one coat hanger per person. Bend the hangers (the hook part) slightly so that they are more straight. Take some kite string and tie it around each person, through the middle of the hanger and just under the armpits. The hanger should be hanging on the person's back. Then make a ring out of another hanger. Any size will do—the smaller the ring, the harder the game becomes. (You'll probably need some pliers to bend the hanger into a ring.) Line up the teams, and in relay fashion pass the ring from person to person, using only the hanger on each person's back to pass it with. No hands are allowed. It takes real coordination.

HOOK UP

An active game, Hook-up works best with ten or more people. Divide into pairs, then have the partners link elbows and form a circle of pairs with at least four feet separating each pair from another. Then choose one person to be the "chaser" and another to be the "chasee." The chaser attempts to tag the chasee while running inside, outside, and weaving through the circle of pairs. The chasee, anytime he wants to, can "pull into the pits" by grabbing the free elbows of one of the pairs. Doing so makes the chasee safe and takes him out of the chase while making the person on the other side of the one whose elbow he grabbed the chasee. If the chasee is tagged, he becomes the chaser and the chaser becomes the chasee.

HOT TOWEL

Here's an active indoor game. Everyone sits in a circle, except one person in the center of the circle who is "it." "It" tosses a towel to someone sitting in the circle, and then the towel is passed around the circle in either direction. The object of the game is for "it" to tag whoever is holding the towel *while it is in their possession*. The towel keeps moving, which makes this very difficult, unless someone is having trouble getting rid of it. If it is passed to you, you must take it. Part of the fun is when someone passes the towel by looping it around the next person's neck or arm, which makes it hard to undo in a hurry. If you are tagged with the towel, then you are the next "it."

HOW THE WEST WAS FUN

Here's an exciting game for camps. Divide into four (or more) teams. Give each team different colored armbands. Each player also gets a masking tape (or adhesive tape) "scalp", which can be placed on each person's forehead. Each tape scalp should be marked with an initial or some other mark that identifies the team. The teams are: the Cowboys, the Indians, the Miners, and the Outlaws. If you have more teams, then just invent more western-style names and expand the rules to include them.

The object of the game is to find bags of gold and return them to the bank, and also to "kill" people (capture scalps). The bags of gold (rocks painted with gold paint) are hidden prior to the game all over the playing area in difficult-to-find places. Just before the game starts, everybody spreads out over the area. Then the whistle or horn blows, indicating that the game is on. You get 1000 points for every scalp you collect (people you "kill"), but:

> Cowboys may only kill Outlaws.
> Indians may only kill Cowboys.
> Miners may only kill Indians.
> Outlaws may only kill Miners.

Anyone who kills a player from the wrong team is automatically dead himself. Boys can only kill boys, but girls can kill anybody. Once your scalp is gone, you are temporarily out of the game. You must go to "Boot Hill" for five minutes; then you may get a new scalp and reenter the game.

If a bag of gold is found, it must go to the "bank" before you get points for it. A bag of gold is worth 5000 points. Players may steal the gold while it is on its way to the bank. Any method of stealing the gold is legal. But again, boys can't steal the gold from girls. No player may come within fifty yards of the bank unless he is carrying the gold or is chasing someone who is. The game is over when the time limit is up or when all the bags of gold have been found and turned in for points. The team with the most points is the winner. Another twist is to hide one bag of "fool's gold" (non-painted rocks or rocks with some secret marking on them). Any team that brings it in loses 5000 points.

HUMAN CROQUET

This game is played much like the regular version of croquet, only using people instead of a croquet set. Set up five or nine people as the croquet "markers," who stand in position according to the diagram below with their legs apart.

25

Line up everyone else into two teams behind the ends (points A and B). The object is to crawl through all the markers (between their legs) on your hands and knees and back to the beginning in a relay race. Each person does it one at a time until everyone on the team has gone. The first team to finish is the winner.

INFILTRATION

Infiltration is a great game to play at camps. It should be played after dark in an area where there are no artificial lights. It is also best played in a wooded area.

Initial set-up: A perimeter is designated along easily recognizable objects (i.e., trees, fallen logs, rocks, etc.). The radius should be between 70 and 100 yards, depending upon the size of the group. A flag is placed in the center of the perimeter. The group is divided into two teams: the defenders and the infiltrators.

Object: It is the goal of the "infiltrators" to sneak into the area inside the perimeter, obtain the flag, and sneak out without being "killed." It is the object of the defenders to prevent any infiltrator from taking the flag.

Equipment: All defenders will need flashlights. (The type with a button that allows short "bursts" of light is best.) And something designated as a flag is needed.

Rules for the Defenders

1. No defender may enter the perimeter.
2. The defenders "kill" an infiltrator by "shooting" him with his flashlight. The flashlights may not be on for more than one second per shot. (No using the flashlights as searchlights.)
3. Any defender using his flashlight as a searchlight or repeatedly firing his flashlight will be "out of ammo" for five minutes.
4. Once a defender believes that he has a "kill," he may keep his flashlight positioned on the spot where he believes his victim is. A judge will check to see if there is anyone there. (The beam must be on the victim.)

Rules for the Infiltrators

1. Once an infiltrator knows that he is "shot," he must stand up and identify himself (i.e., "Smith, dead.").
2. Once killed, the infiltrator then goes back to a designated area. A judge is to be stationed in this area. The infiltrator is kept there for five minutes and then allowed to reenter the game.
3. If an infiltrator believes that the defender does not know exactly where he is, then he may wait silently until a judge comes to determine whether the defender's beam is on him.
4. The infiltrator can be "killed" inside or outside the perimeter.

Judges: This game requires two judges. One judge is located outside the perimeter in the "infiltrators' cemetery." His job is to time the period the infiltrators are out of the game. He keeps them there for five minutes.

The other judge is located inside the perimeter. His responsibility is to check out any disputed "kills." He does this by going to the spot where the defender's flashlight beam is located. He declares the infiltrator dead if he is within the beam. He also declares any defender "out of ammo" who uses his flashlight as a searchlight (either as a steady beam or a rapid series of short bursts). It is best to give the defender a warning before declaring him out of ammo. The defender is out of ammo for five minutes, then is allowed to resume play.

Winning the game: At the beginning a time limit is set. The infiltrators win if they capture the flag before the time expires. The defenders win if they protect their flag the entire time.

INNER TUBE ROLL RELAY

This challenging game can be played indoors or out. Divide the group into teams with an even number of people on each team. Then each team has its members pair up. The first couple from each team stands behind the starting line. A large inflated inner tube (preferably an inner tube from a bus or truck tire) is placed on the floor between them. At the sound of the whistle the couple must stand the tube up and together roll it around a chair and back to the starting line without using their hands. If the inner tube falls while they are rolling it, they must come back to the starting line and begin again. They are not allowed to kick the inner tube along in a lying down position. When the couple successfully completes their round trip, the next couple places the tube flat on the floor, and without using their hands they stand it up and "keep on tubin'." The first team to have all its couples successfully complete the relay is the winner. If a team does not have an even number, someone can go twice. The couples do not need to be of the opposite sex.

MUSICAL SQUIRT GUN

This exciting game can be played with a group ranging from six to thirty, indoors or out. Have the group sit in a circle either on chairs or on the floor. A "loaded" squirt gun is passed around the circle until the music stops or until the leader says, "Stop." The person who is holding the squirt gun at that time must leave the game. But before he leaves, he may squirt the person on his left twice or on his right twice or one each. After his chair is removed, the circle moves in a bit and the game continues. The last person left is declared the winner.

Note: The gun must be passed with two hands and received with two hands or else it will be dropped frequently and will break. Also, it works best to have a second "loaded" squirt gun on hand to be substituted for the one which becomes empty. An assistant can then refill the original gun while the second one is being used. Be sure to emphasize that only two squirts are allowed. Otherwise you will be continually refilling the squirt guns. This is an exciting game. As teens are eliminated, they will be "gunnin'" for a particular person and you will not be able to "water down" the excitement.

27

NEW MODIFIED VOLLEYBALL

This game is played on a regulation volleyball court, with the same rules for scoring and boundaries. However, the rules for play and the strategy are quite different from the traditional game of volleyball. The following modifications make the game playable for those less skilled in the techniques of volleyball, and provide a new challenge for the experience volleyball player.

1. Each team may have four to twelve players.
2. On each volley, a team is allowed five hits and two bounces (on the floor or ground) of the ball on their side of the court.
3. The game is played without a net. A mark on the poles that would hold a net, or on a wall, will indicate the height that the ball must reach on each volley. This should be about the height of the tallest player.
4. Teams cannot cross over the center court line.
5. There is no spiking.
6. An individual player may hit the ball no more than twice in succession. If a player hits the ball, then allows it to bounce once or twice, he/she can hit the ball only once more before another player must hit it. In other words, bounces don't interrupt the succession of hits by a player.
7. Any person in the back line may serve the ball.
8. Rotation is encouraged but not necessary.

Alternative suggestion: If each team is required to use five hits and two bounces on each volley, more players will be involved in the game and additional strategy will develop.

OFFICIAL 43-MAN SQUAMISH

Here's a crazy game that's a lot of fun to play. It's from an old edition of *Mad* magazine, and it is published here with the permission of *Mad's* publisher, William Gaines.

The Field: Squamish will obviously be played on the Squamish field. The boundaries will be set by the LUNKHEAD.

Equipment: One, two, three, or four balls may be used. Two (2, too, to) goals (known as the FURD), one on each end of the field, are used.

Object: To get the ball through the FURD.

The Rules:

    A. *The Ball:*   The ball may be kicked (the GROTZ), carried (the EMPHLE), or thrown (the SLAM).

          1. The GROTZ . . . must be done with the left foot (unless the player is left footed, in which case it will be done with the right foot). If it is done with the right, this will be called a RABBLE GROTZ. Penalty . . . the loss of one man for two (2) minutes.

2. The EMPHLE . . . must be done with two hands. If done with one, this will be called a RABBLE EMPHLE. Penalty . . . loss of one man for one (1) minute.
3. The SLAM is done with two hands. If done with one, it is a RABBLE SLAM. Penalty: the loss of one man for one minute.

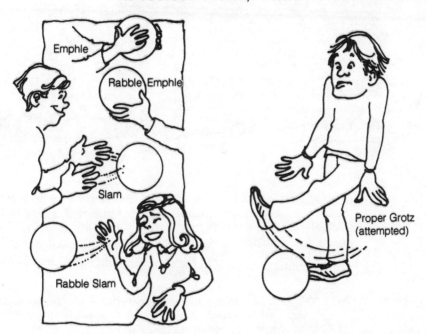

B. *The Tackle:* Tackling the player who has the ball is legal. This is called the SQUAMISH PLAY, but must be preceded with the cry ORG!

1. A man who SQUAMISHES without an ORG has committed a RABBLE SQUAMISH. Penalty . . . leave the game for one (1) minute.
2. The SQUAMISHER may not take the ball from one who has been SQUAMISHED. This must be done by another player.
3. An unnecessarily rough SQUAMISH will force the ejection of the SQUAMISHER.

C. *Scoring:* The only legal way to get a ball through the FURD is with the GROTZ. You may not use the EMPHLE or the SLAM to score.

D. *Goalies:* Two men, GREMLES, may protect the FURD. If more than two GREMLES are used, the FURD GREMLES must remain out of the game for one (1) minute.

A CLASSIC SQUAMISH

E. *Officials:*   If an official, TUNKEN, calls a RABBLE, the player who is RAB-BLED must report to the RABBLE ROUSER. He will be told by the official timer, the RABBLE ROUSER, when to enter the game again. Overall supervision is by the LUNKHEAD. TUNKENS and the LUNKHEAD have final word. The LUNKHEAD may make up his own rules as the game progresses.

Remember: SQUAMISH is the true and elite sportsman's game and should be played with dignity. (In accordance with the 43-man SQUAMISH rules, in MAD MAGAZINE.)

(Contributed by George H. Butler, Detroit, Michigan; ©1965 by E.C. Publications, Inc.)

OJII-SAN TO OBAA-SAN

Here's a fun game from Japan. The players sit in a circle, and two rolled-up kerchiefs are given to any two players in the circle who are seated some distance apart. One kerchief represents the grandmother (Ojii-san) and the other kerchief represents the grandfather (Obaa-san). The game is built around the idea that the grandmother is chasing the grandfather. Here's how it works:

When the game starts, the players who have the kerchiefs put them around their necks, tie a simple overhand knot, give their hands one clap, then pull the kerchiefs off and pass them to the players on their right who repeat the same process. This process continues until someone gets caught with the grandmother kerchief before he/she succeeds in passing the grandfather kerchief on the next player. Whoever gets caught receives a penalty of some kind.

ONE-HANDED CRAZY VOLLEYBALL

Crazy Volleyball is a great game if you don't have quite enough kids to get up a "real" volleyball game. Another problem faced frequently is what to do if you have more than eighteen players (nine on a side). The solution is simple but challenging: Allow the players to use only one hand and play by "Crazy Volleyball" rules:

1. Each team is allowed to hit the ball four times before it goes over the net.
2. If a ball hits the floor or the ground it counts as one hit.
3. A ball cannot hit the floor twice in succession.
4. Players may use only one hand to hit the ball.

With these rules more than the traditional eighteen people may play volleyball. In fact, twenty-four to thirty is not too many to play the game. This game may be played either indoors or out. The more players you have, the further back you can make the back out-of-bounds line.

OVER THE LINE

Here's a great softball game that has become popular on Southern California beaches in recent years. All that is needed is a bat and a softball, six people (three on a team), and some way to mark the boundaries of the playing field, which looks like this:

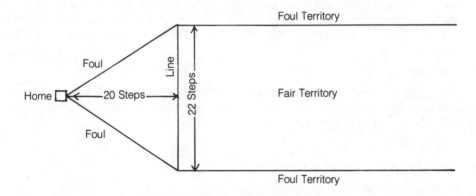

The batter of the team that is up stands at home plate and tries to hit the ball over the line (in the air) in fair territory. The ball is pitched from someone from the same team (the team that is up) in one of two ways: (a) The "official" way is for the pitcher to kneel on the other side of home plate, opposite the batter, and toss the ball straight up for the batter to hit. This is the way it is normally done although it tends to be dangerous.

(b) The pitch may also be delivered in the conventional manner with the pitcher standing fifteen or twenty feet from the batter (anywhere he wants) and lobbing the ball up to be hit. The disadvantage is that it is harder to get a hit this way. The pitcher cannot interfere with the ball after it is hit or the batter is out.

The team in the field position themselves in fair territory (anywhere they want). If they catch a hit ball before it hits the ground, the batter is out. Any ball that drops into fair territory on the fly is a base hit. A ball hit in fair territory over the heads of all three fielders is a home run.

There are no bases, so no base running. The bases are imaginary. When a person gets a base hit, the next batter comes up and hits. It takes three base hits (not four as in regular softball) before a run is scored, then every base hit after that adds on another run. A home run after the first three base hits would score four runs (clearing the bases, plus one bonus run) and it takes three more base hits to start scoring runs again. Other rules:

1. Each batter gets only two pitches to get a hit (only one foul, missed swing, etc.). If you don't get a hit in two pitches, you are out.
2. Any ball hit on the ground in front of the line is an out. (Unless it's foul on the first pitch.)
3. Each team gets three outs per inning, as in regular softball.
4. The game is played for nine innings (or as many as you want).

Of course, the rules of the game may be modified as you wish. For example, the boundaries can be adjusted to fit the skills of the players. Or instead of using a softball, you could use a mush ball or a volleyball. You could play with more (or less) on a team. It is great on the sand at the beach as well as on a regular playing field. Be creative and have fun.

OVER THE LINE II

Here's a slightly more complicated version of the previous game. The playing field, the three-person teams, and the other rules remain much the same with a few modifications. For example, the field has two more lines:

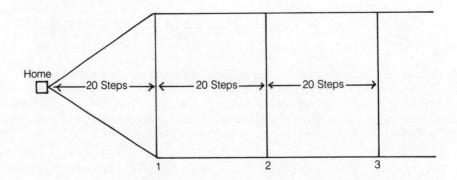

If the batter hits the ball between lines 1 and 2, it counts as a single; between lines 2 and 3 is a *double;* over line 3 is a *triple;* and over the head of the last opposing player is a *home run.* Again the defending players may play anywhere they want in the field, but usually it is best to have one player defending each of the three territories.

The scoring is exactly like regular baseball, but all runs must be *forced* home. For instance, if there is a man on first and second (base runners are still imaginary—nobody really runs) and the next batter hits a double, then one run scores. Now there are men on second and third. If the next one hits a single, nobody scores since first base is open. Another single would score a run, since the bases would be loaded.

Usually singles, doubles, and triples are counted as such only when the ball crosses the appropriate line in the air. However, for more excitement and larger scores, try this: A single must land behind line 1 on the fly (as usual), but if the fielder lets it roll or bounce past line 2 in fair territory, then it is a double, even though it hit the ground in single territory. Same thing with a triple. If the ball crosses the third line, no matter how it got there, it counts as a triple. Home runs are still the same—over the head of everybody. All other rules are the same as regular Over the Line.

PYRAMID RACE

Teams of six players build three-level pyramids and race to a point. If a pyramid collapses, they must stop and rebuild it.

ROLLER BASKETBALL

Using an outdoor basketball court, two teams on roller skates attempt to score points by hitting the opponent's backboard with a beachball. (Teams can have between five and ten players each.) Players may either carry the ball or tap it as in volleyball. If a player is tagged by an opponent while carrying the ball, it goes over to the other team. The ball is put into play by passing it in from out of bounds. A "foul" gives the opposing team a free throw from the basketball free throw line.

ROOFBALL

For this game, you will need a volleyball and a roof. Experimentation will tell which roofs are the best. The unique thing about roofball is that each roof produces a new challenge, a different twist to the game. Decide on the out-of-bounds, then form a single-file line perpendicular to the line of the roof. First in line serves the ball up on the roof and moves to the back of the line. Second in line must play the ball by hitting the ball (volleyball-style) back onto the roof (before it hits the ground). He then moves to the back of the line, with the third player playing the ball. This continues until a miss or until a played ball lands out-of-bounds.

Missed balls are those that don't make it to the roof, are hit under the roofline, go over the roof, are completely missed, are played while the player is in contact with the ground, or land out-of-bounds. Obviously, the player who is responsible for the ball's going out is charged with the miss. When you miss three times, you are out of the game, and the game continues until there is just one person left who is the winner.

To play with teams, form two lines, one for each team. The first player on Team One hits the ball up onto the roof, and the first player on Team Two hits it up again, then back to the second person on Team One, and so on. Every time somebody misses, the other team gets points.

ROOT BEER RELAY

This is especially good on a hot day but is fun anytime. Divide into teams. Each player gets a straw. On tables in front of the lined-up teams are large pots of ice-cold, highly carbonated root beer. At the starting whistle, the first players on each team run to the pots of root beer with their straws and begin drinking. Every ten seconds the referee blows a whistle, and the next players in line run up and drink (first players go to the end of the line). The team to finish the last drop of root beer wins. Players may have to go several times in turn before the race is over.

SABOTAGE WATER WAR

Give each player a large plastic cup full of water and have them spread out over an area the size of a basketball court. They hold their cups in their left hands and try to upset other players' cups with their right hands. They may not throw the water at anyone; they may only try to knock the water out of each other's cups. The last one to remain on the court with some water in his cup wins.

SCARECROW STUFF

This game is great for a Halloween party or a hayride where plenty of hay or straw is available. Divide the kids into two or more teams depending on the size of the group. Each team should have an equal size pile of hay before them. Each team chooses a person to serve as the team's "scarecrow." The "scarecrows" must stand the same distance away wearing oversized overalls. The object will be to see which team can use up all their hay in stuffing their "scarecrow." For added laughs have the "scarecrows" finish the race by running to a finish line.

SHARK IN THE DARK

This is a simple water game. The object is for swimmers to swim through "shark-infested" waters without being attacked.

The swimming area has two safety points twenty feet apart. Appoint one youth to be the "shark." The shark waits near one end of the swimming area; the rest of the swimmers are at the other end. At a given signal, the shark submerges and all of the swimmers head for the opposite safety area. The shark must move and make all attacks while swimming under water. The shark must bring his victim's shoulders out of the water to constitute a legal attack. Sharks may stop and surface for air and to look for victims as needed.

All of the swimmers who were attacked now become sharks for the next round. It is important to pause a moment so your sharks and swimmers can position themselves before you signal the next round to begin. This allows time for the sharks to rest and plan their strategy.

As the game progresses you should have more sharks and fewer swimmers. The last swimmer attacked is the winner. The first one attacked becomes the shark for the next game. The game works best in a lake in four to five feet of water, although a pool is satisfactory.

SHOE BOX RELAY

Here's a great idea for an "Olympics Night." Find several shoe boxes, a high school track, and a referee. Divide the kids into teams. Have them place their feet into the boxes and then "hoof it" around the track. You may want to divide into several stations. You may need plenty of replacement shoe boxes in case they wear out quickly. You should experience a hilarious situation.

SHUFFLE YOUR BUNS AGAIN

Everyone sits in a circle, and each has a chair to sit on. There are two "its," in the middle of the circle and only one extra chair in the circle. On "go," the two people who are "it" try to outmaneuver each other to sit in the extra chair. The kids in the circle keep moving from seat to seat trying to protect the extra chair, because if one of the two "its" sits in the chair, whoever is to his or her right joins the other "it" in the middle of the circle for the next round.

SNEAKO CREEPO

This is a night game, and you will need a building with a large flat roof and one or two entrance doors. Two players are selected to go up on top of the roof with flashlights or lanterns; everyone else has two minutes to hide away from the building (at least 100 feet) in the grass, behind bushes, in trash cans, etc. On a signal, players on the ground try to sneak and creep into the building without being seen. Players on the roof search with their flashlights and call out the names of whoever they see. The first two to make it in get to be on the roof for the next round.

SNOW PENTATHLON

Here's a wild event for your next "Winter Olympics" or snow retreat. Divide into teams of eight, and have the following five events set up. Teams must compete in each event to achieve the best time. The teams proceed from one event to the next. Some of these games may be a little rough, so be sure they are well supervised to insure safety. You may want to change the rules slightly in some cases if they seem too difficult for your group.

1. *Stand-up-and-go:* The eight team members are tied tightly together at the waist to form a circle. They begin by sitting on the snow facing out. At the sound of the whistle they must all stand up together without touching the snow with their hands.
2. *Slalom:* Remaining tied together in a circle they must pass through the starting gate and run (or walk) through a slalom course marked with ski poles. They must pass on alternate sides of each successive ski pole. If a ski pole is knocked down, the team must return to the starting gate and begin again.
3. *Tubecide:* The team may now untie between two of the team members and stretch out in a straight line. They are given two inner tubes which they must take to the top of the tubing run and come down the run as a team on the two tubes. Use caution on this one if the run is quite steep or fast as someone could be dragged quite a distance if they fall off a tube.
4. *Hill Roll:* Remaining hooked together in a straight line, the team must now travel from the top of a small hill to the bottom of the hill without standing on their feet. At the bottom they may stand up and untie from each other.
5. *Octa-ski:* Two 2 x 6 pieces of lumber each have short rope loops attached to them at one-foot intervals. Each team member must place a foot through a loop on each "ski," then the team skis the final 200 feet to the finish line.

Usually we soon forget who won the event but we do remember the teamwork, competitive spirit, and effort which are more important than winning anyway.

SPACE WAR

Here's a game that works best with teams of 50–75 each. Be sure you use good balloons that do not break easily. This game is a lot of fun!

There are two teams: the Rebels (orange ballons) and the Galactic Empire (green balloons). The Rebels are led by Luke Skywaddler and are divided into small groups, each commanded by a Sky Colonel. The Galactic Forces are commanded by the dreaded Derth Vector and are likewise divided into small groups, each led by a Space Commander. The battlefield consists of a very large area (campground, etc.) that is divided into two spaces. In the Rebel Space there will be five clearly identified and well-spaced Air Bases and one P.O.W. area. From these five Air Bases the Rebels will launch their attack. In the Galactic Empire Space there are five clearly identified and well-spaced Life Control Receptacles (L.C.R.'s) and one P.O.W. camp. The L.C.R.'s can be ordinary garbage cans. Each player should have a green or orange balloon attached (tied) to his or her wrist. These are known as Life Support Tanks.

The objective of the game is to destroy the enemy by "de-lifing" enemy soldiers, destroying Air Bases, bombing L.C.R.'s de-lifing either Derth Vector or Luke Skywaddler, and thus making as many points as possible in the 45 minutes of play. The rules and instructions below should be given to each player.

Points are awarded as follows:

1. 100 points for each enemy soldier de-lifed and carried to your team's P.O.W. area.
2. 500 points for each Air Base or Life Control Receptacle destroyed.
3. 1000 points for de-lifing and carrying to your team's P.O.W. area either Derth Vector or Luke Skywaddler.

Team with the most points after penalties wins!

General Rules of Play:

1. All combat is by hand only. You de-life opponent by popping his or her balloon. No tripping, shoving, tackling, strangling, or holding allowed. The second your balloon is popped you are dead.
2. Once you are de-lifed that's it. You are dead weight until the end of the game.
3. If you want to get points for de-lifed enemy soldiers, you must carry or drag them to your team's P.O.W. area. Boys can only drag or carry boys. Girls can only drag or carry girls.
4. Rebel bombs destroy Galactic Life Control Receptacles by either dropping or throwing a bomb into this container before being delifed. Game Judge at the site will be judge of this. No attempt can be made to move or displace Life Control Receptacle. No attempt can be made to block or bat away bomb once it is thrown. The only defense allowed is to de-life bombs. Once the L.C.R. has been successfully bombed, It is turned upside down. Note: Bombs can be yellow balloons—one given to each Rebel.
5. The Galactic forces destroy Rebel Air Bases by gaining control of the official Air Base sign and tearing it in half before being de-lifed. This sign can in no way be held or touched by Rebel forces.
6. Neither team can employ the defense or offense of a "human ring" or wall around or against an Air Base or L.C.R. by joining hands or locking arms. Each player must be a free agent at all times.
7. Derth Vector and Luke Skywaddler have two balloons, one on each wrist. Both of these must be destroyed if either of these men is to be immobilized.
8. All buildings are off limits.
9. If your balloon accidentally pops—too bad!

Penalties:

1. 100 points per incident of failing to fall dead immediately after your balloon has popped.
2. 300 points per incident for unnecessary roughness.
3. 300 points per incident for failure to obey a Game Judge immediately. Judges will be watching all activity. It will do you no good to accuse or complain about enemy activity.

Good Luck and May The Force Be With You!

SPIDER

A strong player stoops in a tight tuck position with his hands clasped behind his knees. Two volunteers have thirty seconds to try and stretch him out. No slugging or tickling allowed!

STRENGTHBALL RELAYS

The only equipment needed for these relays is one ball that bounces for each team and one basketball goal, or a target, for the game. All teams shoot at the same goal. The starting point should be the same distance from the goal for all teams. The playing area should be set up as follows (the path of each team is indicated by the arrows):

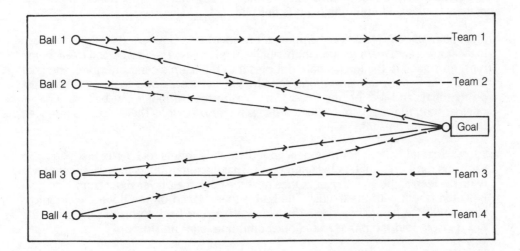

The teams should sit on the floor, with each player standing only to do his/her part. When each player is finished, he/she should sit down in line. No interference with the balls is allowed by those in line. The team that is seated and finished first wins. The following rules apply to the types of Strengthball Relays that can be played:

Piggyback Strengthball: Team members pair off. One partner takes a piggyback position on the other partner's shoulders. On signal, the first pair in line piggyback to the other end of the room, where the team's balls are sitting on the floor. The bottom partner picks up the ball for his/her team and passes it up to the partner riding piggyback. The pair proceed to the goal with the upper partner dribbling the ball. Upon arriving at the goal, the upper partner attempts to score a goal (or hit the designated target) while still riding piggyback. The pair remains at the goal until they achieve one score. Then they return the ball to the other end of the floor (where it was originally picked up) with the upper partner again dribbling the ball. Once the ball is placed, not thrown or dropped, in its original spot, the pair returns to their team. A tag is made to the next pair in line and they repeat this process. The team to finish first faints from exhaustion.

Wheelbarrow Strengthball: Team members pair off. The familiar wheelbarrow positions are assumed by the first pair in each line (back person holds up the feet of the front person, who then walks on his/her hands). On the signal, the first pair proceeds to their team's ball, in wheelbarrow fashion. The ball is corralled by the front person and guided with head and shoulders (no hands) to the goal (target). When the pair arrives under the goal, the back person lets go of the front person's legs. The back person must score one goal. After scoring, the pair returns the ball to its original spot, wheelbarrow style, then returns to their line. A tag is made to the next pair and the process is repeated until one team is finished.

Chair Strengthball: (Additional equipment needed: one chair per team, placed close to the goal.) Team members run individually in this relay. The first person in each line runs, on signal, to the team's ball, dribbles it to the team's chair in front of the goal (target), sits in the chair, and shoots until he/she has scored one goal (must have seat on the chair and feet on the floor). The person then dribbles the ball back to its original spot, runs back to the line, and tags the next person. The process is repeated until one team finishes.

Soccer Strengthball: Team members go individually in this relay. The first person in each line runs, on signal, to the team's ball. That person dribbles the ball soccer-style (with the feet) to the goal (target). Once near the goal, the player shoots until one goal is scored (shoot with the hands). The ball is then placed on the floor and dribbled, soccer-style, to its original spot. The player then runs back to his/her line, tags the next person, and the process continues until one team finishes.

SURPRISE MUSICAL CHAIRS

For this game, you'll need chairs, paper bags, and balloons. Arrange the chairs for a regular game of musical chairs, only there should be enough chairs for everyone, rather than the usual one chair missing. Blow up balloons, put them inside the paper bags, close the bags and place one on each chair. One of the sacks, however, should contain a water balloon. The kids march around the chairs, and when the music stops (or on a signal) everyone sits down in a chair on top of the paper bag. Whoever gets the water balloon is out. Leaders can then set up the chairs again with more bags, and so on, until there is one person left. Obviously, this will take a lot of bags. If you would like to avoid that, have more of the bags contain water balloons, and eliminate more kids the first time around. You can do the same with succeeding rounds also. Make sure the kids aren't watching while the chairs are being "armed."

SWINGER

This is a great game for all ages and is lots of fun to watch as well as play. Take a small (15-inch) drain plunger handle and put a plunger on each end. Then take a small jack ball and 12–15 inches of string and attach the string to the ball with a stright pin. Tie the loose end of the string to the middle of the handle so the ball and string hang from the center.

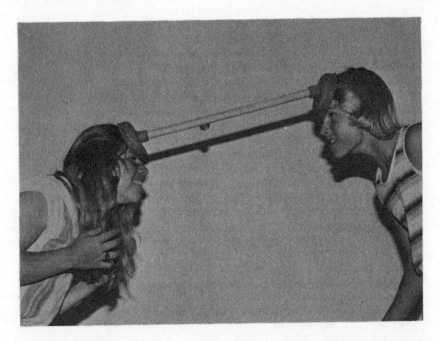

Have couples stand face to face with the rubber plungers resting on their foreheads and their hands behind their backs. With only body movement, the couple has to start the ball swinging and try to flip it over the handle. Time each couple. The couple having the shortest time wins. You might want to set a maximum time in case some just can't do it.

THREE-WAY GIANT BASKETBALL

Instead of two teams for basketball, why not three? All three teams have seven players on the court at a time and at least three of them must be girls. Each team can have up to two "giants" (a la chicken-fight-style) but a girl must be one of the two people comprising the giant. Teams can score at either basket. A player cannot dribble more than two times. Every time a girl scores it's worth five points; a boy scoring is worth two points. Three fouls on anyone and he is out of the game. Be sure to substitute freely so that everyone can play.

TOUCHDOWN TENNIS

This game is simply touch football with tennis rackets and tennis balls. The quarterback uses a tennis racket; the ball is centered to the quarterback who hits the ball to any teammate. Regular rules of touch football apply. A player can catch only one pass in a series of downs and three completes give a first down. Kickoffs are done with the tennis racket. Defense players may rush only after counting to ten. The racket cannot be exchanged during a play.

TUBE-A-LOON RELAY

The Tube-a-loon Relay can be done any one of three ways, depending on the agility of the group involved.

Easy Version: This game is played by placing a number of balloons at one end of a room or route and the team members at the other. Between them you place one, two, or three inner tubes. At the whistle a team member goes and gets a balloon and returns to the line and the next person repeats the process. However, the persons must go through the inner tubes both going and coming.

Tougher Version: This game is a bit more difficult and cozy. The teams are divided up into pairs. At the sound of the whistle the pair (holding hands) must go through the tubes without letting go of each other, pick up a balloon and place it between them (no hands), and return to the line going back through the inner tubes. It is important to have tubes that are large enough and not overinflated.

"Professional" Version: This time put a balloon at the end of the room for each team member. At the whistle the first person goes through the tubes, gets a balloon, and returns back through the tubes. Leaving the balloon at the starting line, he then picks up the next person (not literally, but holding hands) and repeats the course. The process is repeated until the entire team is going after the last balloon. Team members are *not* allowed to let go of hands at any time.

TYPHOON

Here is a relay game that is ideal for summer. Have two lines, single file, facing a water source. At a signal the first person in each line runs to the water, fills a bucket, runs back to his team, and throws the water in the face of his teammate. Before the person can throw the water, his teammate must point and yell, "Typhoon." Each person takes the bucket down to the water and returns to storm his team. The first line to finish is declared the winner.

For safety reasons the participants should be at least three feet from those to receive the water, and a plastic bucket should be used. On a hot day you will be surprised how many times the youth will want to play this game.

WATER BASEBALL

Water Baseball is a great camp game or summer game where everyone can have fun. The only equipment needed are a whiffle ball and plastic bat and a swimming pool. The game is played just like regular baseball except for the few minor changes listed below.

1. There are only two bases plus home plate (diving board).
2. Each team has four infielders (pitcher, first and second basemen, and catcher). Everyone else on the team is in the field (shallow water). The catcher, by the way, should be a good swimmer.

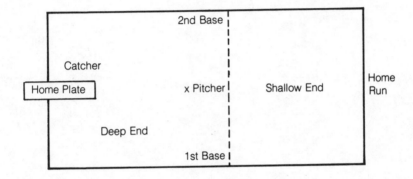

If you are using a larger pool, then the right and left sides of the pool are out-of-bounds and any ball hit there is a foul ball. Balls hit over the far end of the pool are home runs. If the pool is small, however, then anything hit out of the pool is an automatic out.

WATERLOGGED VOLLEYBALL

This game is also great for hot summer days. Put a pole in the middle of the volleyball net with a sprinkler at the top and the hose hooked to the pole. Then just play a regular game of volleyball. If you are playing on the grass be aware of the possible damage that will occur to the grass. This game would best be played on a dirt surface that will get nice and muddy.

WHIFFLE GOLF

Here's a crazy version of golf that kids will enjoy. Set up your own golf course, anywhere you have room. It can be on an open field, all over a campground, around houses—just about anywhere. Each hole is a small tin can or jar just big enough for a whiffle ball to go into. The cans can be placed on the ground and anchored there, or they can be elevated on poles. After the course is set, each player gets a whiffle ball, and "tees-off" for hole number one (there can be nine or eighteen holes). No clubs are used. You simply toss the ball underhanded. Each toss counts as a stroke. The idea is to get the ball into the can in the fewest strokes possible. It is best to play in foursomes, just like regular golf, and by setting a "par" for each hole, printing up scorecards, etc. You can have a Whiffle Golf Tournament just like the pros. If you can't get whiffle balls, you can substitute bean-bags.

Crowd Breakers

Crowd Breakers

BAGPIPES

This really can't be called a song, but it's fun enough not to matter. Divide your group into three sections. The first section sings "Oh" continuously, while lightly hitting their Adam's apples with the side of their hands. The second group sings "Ah" and rhythmically pinches their noses, giving both a straight and nasal tone. The third group holds their noses and to the tune of "The Campbells Are Coming," an old Scottish tune, sings, using the "da" sound. Done correctly, this really does sound like bagpipes, provided the kids can keep from laughing.

BOGGLE MIXER

Divide your young people into small groups. The members of each small group write their first names in large letters on a single piece of paper, one name under the other with a uniform left margin:

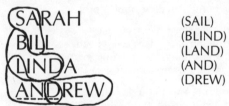

(SAIL)
(BLIND)
(LAND)
(AND)
(DREW)

Each group then tries to make as many words as possible from the combined letters of the names. The words must have three or more letters each. One bonus point is given for five-letter words, two bonus points for six-letter words, etc. Any combination of letters may be used as long as the letters are not contingent to each other. (Proper names and foreign words are not permissible.) Set a three-minute time limit.

CAREER GUESS

If you're planning a "careers night" with your youth group, try this as an icebreaker. Put up a large sheet of paper for each person present. (If you don't have enough wall space, tape the sheets to the tops of tables.) Write each person's name at the top of each sheet and then give everybody a magic marker. Each person should go to every sheet except his/her own and write the occupation that he/she thinks that person will or should be in after his/her education is completed. (Any criterion is ok.) After everyone is finished, each person should write his/her own projected career on that sheet of paper.

CHRISTMAS GROUP DRAMATICS

Here's an audience participation activity that can be a lot of fun. Divide the audience into six groups. Each group should be given a word and a corresponding response. Then the following poem should be read (see below). Every time a group's word is mentioned, they must respond with the correct phrase.

Santa: "Ho, Ho, Ho!"
Reindeer: "Clippity Clop"
Rudolph: "Beep, Beep" (while pinching nose)
Bells: "Jingle, Jingle"
Snow: "Br-r-r-r-r-r"
Sleigh: "Wheeeeee!"

One time long ago in a fake little town
A happening happened and the story's told 'round
How a reindeer named Rudolph was of no help to Santa
Delivering presents in this town near Atlanta.

The sleigh owned by Santa was loaded with presents
By the elves and the reindeer and a large group of peasants.
The reindeer were harnessed with bells on their toes,
But Rudolph must stay home (because of his nose).

Santa, the reindeer, and the sleigh were all ready
To deliver the presents when a problem quite heady
Developed. It stopped them; they just couldn't go.
The problem, you see, was a large storm of snow.

The snow came so hard that Santa couldn't see.
The reindeer wouldn't know where to pull the sleigh.
The reindeer, bells jingling, and Santa made tracks
Through the snow to see Rudolph, a question to ask.

"Rudolph," said Santa and the reindeer in unison,
"If this snow stops us this year our act is for sure done.
We've a sleigh full or presents to deliver tonight,
And the snow is so heavy, we have little sight.

"Will you and your nose guide the reindeer to housetops
So that Santa with presents can make all of his stops?
Rudolph yawned and looked out at the wind-driven snow
And said, "Santa and reindeer, I just cannot go.

48

"The sleigh is too heavy with presents delightful,
But if you ask me, the job seems a might dull.
Besides, all this snow and your bells out of tune,
The cold is too much. Ask again come next June."

GREASEBALL

This game is not only fun, but funny. Give each contestant two plates (preferably tin, paper, or plastic). Have them place the two plates in front of them, side by side. Each contestant counts out twenty-five cotton balls and puts them in the right plate and then puts an adequate supply of Vaseline on their noses. With hands behind their backs the object is to see who can be the first one to move all the cotton balls from the right-hand plate to the left-hand plate without the use of hands or tongue. They can blow or twitch with their noses. Winner receives all the cotton balls and a jar of partially used Vaseline.

THE HEN SHE CACKLES

Place three chairs in front of the group (make sure the middle chair is flat). Explain to the group that you want to do an exercise in communication and will need five volunteers: three to be "mediators" and two to be "arguers" (the arguers have been clued in ahead of time). The five people are chosen and two of the mediators are asked to leave the room because this is an exercise to see who has better skills at mediating. The two arguers are placed on the outside seats with the mediator in the middle chair. The mediator is told to say and do everything that the two on either side say and do. (To make it look unrehearsed, also explain to the arguers what they are supposed to say and do.)

First arguer to mediator: "The hen she cackles." (Mediator relays)

Second arguer to mediator: "What?" (Mediator relays)

First arguer to mediator: "The hen she cackles." (Mediator relays)

Second arguer to mediator: "I don't understand." (Mediator relays)

First arguer to mediator: "Like this." (He gets up and put hands in armpits and acts like a chicken cackling and then sits down.)

When the mediator gets up and starts cackling like a chicken, then one of the two arguers puts an egg on his chair which he promptly sits on. This skit can also be made to backfire on the first arguer by cluing in the mediator to what's going on and handing him an egg.

LOVELY CONFUSION

Here's a good Valentine's Day mixer for groups of twenty-five or more. Give everyone the list as printed below. Each person is on his/her own and the first person to accomplish all ten instructions is the winner. (They do not have to be accomplished in order, but they must all be done.)

1. Get ten different autographs: first, middle, and last names (on the back of this sheet).

2. Unlace someone's shoe, lace it, and tie it again.

3. Find two other people and the three of you form a heart shape lying on the floor.

4. Get a girl to kiss this paper five times and sign her name.

   _____

5. If you are a girl—have a boy get down on his knee and propose to you. If you are a boy—get down on your knee and propose to any girl. Sign his/her name.

   _____

6. Eat ten red hots and show your red tongue to someone you do not know well. They sign here. _____

7. Say this poem as loudly as you can.

   > How do I love thee?
   > Let me count the ways.
   > I love thee to the depth and breadth and height
   > My soul can reach. . . .
   >
   > I love thee to the level of every day's
   > Most quiet need . . .
   > I love thee with the breath,
   > Smiles, tears, of all my life!—and, if God choose,
   > I shall but love thee better after death.

8. Ask ten people to be your valentine and record your score.

   Yes _____ No _____

9. Leap-frog over someone five times.

10. You were given a piece of bubble gum at the beginning of the race. Chew it up and blow five bubbles. Find someone who will watch you do it and sign here when you finish. _____

MATCH UP

Here's a good game that can be used as a crowd breaker or mixer. It really gets people talking and mixing with each other, and it's a lot of fun. Index cards are typed or written with statements like those listed on the next page. The last word or words are typed onto the small right-hand portion of the card, which is then cut off (see illustration).

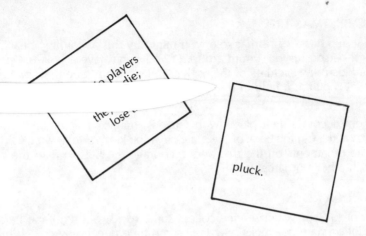

A Sample List of Phrases:

I always eat bacon with *my eggs.*
Tarzan lived in the jungle with his wife *Jane.*
The worth of the American dollar is about *40 cents.*
We could save on gasoline with fewer *"jackrabbit starts."*
What good is a peanut butter sandwich without *peanut butter?*
Speak softly and carry *a big stick.*

The large and small portions of the cards are handed out at random to people with the instructions that they are to find the correct match-up with their portion. They must do this by going up to someone, introducing themselves, and then holding their cards together and reading them out loud. Some combinations can be quite funny. If two people think they have a match, they must go to the designated leader, who has all the correct answers, and check to make sure. If they have a correct match, they may sit down. Another variation is to give everyone a large and small portion of cards (which do not match) and make them find both matches.

NAME COUNT

This is a great game when you have lots of newcomers in the youth group. Have the group form a circle and choose someone to be in the middle. The person in the middle points to anyone, yells "right" or "left," then counts to five as quickly as possible (must be intelligible however). The person who has been pointed to must yell out the person's name on his/her right or left (whichever side was called) before "it" counts to five, otherwise, he/she must be "it." The group should change places occasionally.

POLAROID CHRISTMAS TREE

If your youth group has a Christmas tree, you might try this rewarding idea. Take a picture of each person in your youth group. (If you don't have a polaroid camera, then have the kids bring pictures of themselves.) Have them glue their pictures on small paper plates punch a hole in the top, and put in a piece of yarn to hang the "ornament."

Then have them decorate their plates with crayons, magic markers, and whatever else you can provide. On the back of the plate have the kids write down a Christmas wish. Hang the ornaments on the tree and encourage the kids to read the wishes written on each other's ornaments.

REFLECTIONS IN A ROCK

Some time prior to your youth service collect some rocks, one for each person in your group. Collecting these rocks may take some time depending on the number that will be participating, but it is time well spent. Each rock should, if possible, be quite different in shape, color, roughness, size, etc.

The next step is to form a circle, with your group as close together as possible. Before handing out the rocks, explain in detail the object of this, which would be the introduction for your lesson.

You should explain that each person will receive a rock and that he/she will be given time to examine it in great detail. Then they should ask God what He can show them in their rock that reflects their own life. (Example: The sharp edge on one side of the rock might represent sin in one's life that needs to be smoothed out and, like the water of a swift stream smooths the stone, so might people—parents, youth leaders, etc.—do so in one's life.) You the leader will be pleased as you see youth participate like never before. You'll learn about things in their lives you'd never discover in a counseling discussion or even by being close to them. They'll reflect the past, present, and even future process they feel will have to occur so that God can use them daily.

SPONTANEOUS POETRY

Break into small groups of seven to ten and give each group a piece of paper. The first person in the group writes down a word at the top of the piece of paper and passes it to the next person. The second person contemplates the first word, writes another word just below the first word, and then folds the paper so the first word cannot be seen—only their word is visible. This process is repeated for each person in the group, with each person carefully folding the paper so that only his/her word can be seen. When the last word has been written, the paper is unfolded and the "poem" is read.

A person can write any kind of word and should not spend a lot of time thinking of just the "right" word. The results are hilarious.

STRAWLESS RELAY

Have three or four kids put one end of an ordinary drinking straw into their mouths. Have them all start at the same time and try to get their mouths from one end of the straw to the other without using their hands. The only legal way to do this is by using their mouths and tongues. The facial expressions will have the audience in stitches.

ZIPPITY UP—ZIPPITY DOWN

Have the group sit in a circle with two chairs facing each other in the middle of the circle. Then have some volunteers leave the room. The leader of the game must sit in one chair and the volunteers (brought in one at a time) must sit in the other chair. Each holds a spoon in his/her right hand. The object of the game is for the volunteers to follow the leader's instructions as accurately and as quickly as they can. The leader then begins by moving his right hand with the spoon as far to the right as he can and says, "Zippity right." The volunteer does the exact same thing including saying the words *zippity right*. The leader continues with "zippity left" and repeats both commands until the volunteer is catching on. Then the leader says, "Zippity down," and puts the spoon as far down between his legs as possible. After the volunteer follows, the leader stands up with his right hand extended into the air and says, "Zippity up." The leader continues repeating all four commands until the time is right. Then while the volunteer is doing "zippity up," someone places a water balloon or egg on the volunteer's chair with interesting results.

Creative Communication

Creative Communication

ARMAGEDDON BOMBER

If played seriously, this can be a great discussion starter. Armageddon Bomber is a simulation game that can be done with several groups in different rooms. Each group should include four people (pilot, bombardier, radio controller, and co-pilot). Give the following information to each group:

> The year is 1984. You are the flight team of an advanced, ultramodern U.S. bomber and you are flying maneuvers over the Atlantic. Suddenly you receive a highly classified message which is coded and comes from a computer. (The message below should be given to each flight team in coded form. Make up your own code and give each group the key.)

EMERGENCY ALERT: CODE RED

U.S. HAS RECEIVED NUCLEAR ATTACK BY USSR. CASUALTIES AND DESTRUCTION NOT KNOWN AT THIS TIME. U.S. UNABLE TO RETALIATE. . . . TOTAL DESTRUCTION IS IMMINENT. YOU ARE CARRYING ADVANCED NUCLEAR WARHEAD. ONLY HOPE. YOUR LOCATION PINPOINTED HALFWAY BETWEEN U.S. AND USSR. YOUR FUEL AT 50 PERCENT. MAINTAIN RADIO SILENCE AND PROCEED WITH OPERATION RANGER RED. DELIVER WARHEAD.

Each group has twenty minutes to decode the message and make a decision among themselves. The decision to fulfill the mission must be unanimous. If your team decides *not* to fulfill the mission, your options are as follows:

1. You will change course and attempt to land in Greenland and hope the contamination has not reached you.
2. You will attempt to crash the plane in the target area rather than stay alive.
3. You will surrender to the enemy.
4. You will commit suicide and not drop the bomb.
5. You will simply keep flying and hope that you can get a clear picture of the situation and make up your mind at the last possible minute.
6. You will fly back to the U.S. and assess the damage. And hope that you can refuel somewhere.

After the time is up have each group share its decision and the reasons for it. Here are some possible questions:

1. Do the teachings of Jesus apply to this situation? If so, which ones?
2. How much of your decision was influenced by your Christian convictions?

BACK TO THE GARDEN

This is a youth program/outing designed to improve young people's basic understanding of the Crucifixion and Resurrection events.

First, develop short scripts (scenarios) based on the following scenes:

A. Preparation for Passover (Matt. 26:17–19)
B. In the Upper Room (John 13:1–14:27)
C. Institution of the Lord's Supper (Matt. 26:26–30)
D. At Gethsemane (Matt. 26:36–46)
E. Jesus Arrested (Matt. 26:47–56; Luke 22:47–53; John 18:1–11)
F. Trial by Caiaphas (Matt. 26:57–68; Mark 14:53–65; John 18:19–24)

Select a site that will have a large open room, a meandering path, and several spots along the path where a group can stop and sit. Organize a group of actors (adults and young people) to memorize the scripts and create costumes that reflect the period. The people then arrive in groups and begin their walk to the Garden to relive the Easter events all over again.

1. Near the area where people are brought, present a scene where the disciples are instructed to set up the Lord's Supper.
2. Take group to the "Upper Room" for portrayal of the Last Supper. (At the close of this scene have everyone in the audience also participate in the Lord's Supper.)
3. Continue down the path stopping for the scenes at Gethsemane, Jesus' arrest, and the trial.
4. End the evening by having the group assemble around a large cross (heavy enough so that it takes a number of people to lift it). Give a brief devotional about the Cross, and then close with the entire group attempting to lift the cross together.

COMMERCIAL RELIGION

There's no doubt that commercials influence every aspect of our daily lives. Therefore commercials can be an effective media technique. There are some dangers, however:

1. Commercials tend to entertain rather than inform.
2. Commercials tend to consolidate reality, simplify reality into black-and-white categories.
3. Commercials tend to exaggerate and manipulate.
4. Commercials tend to use symbols.

There are many other dangers when it comes to commercials and it is important that a youth group not accept commercials as valid communication devices nor feel that just by changing one word the entire meaning will change. For example, consider the phrase "Coke adds life" changed to "Christ adds life." True, such statements are catchy, but is the "changed" statement true? In what ways?

But because most people hear commercials all the time, it can be a lot of fun to allow your youth group to make some commercials for God, Christ, or the church by adapting popular commercials, or by creating entirely new ones. Divide your youth group (if possible) into small groups and give them a few minutes to create their own commercial around whatever theme you give them. Give the kids enough time to practice and gather together whatever props they need. Then have the groups present their ideas to each other one at a time. You might tell the group something like this: "You have been given 60 seconds (or 30 seconds) on national prime time television to create and produce a commercial for God, Jesus, or the church. Millions of people will see it. What kind of spot would you create?"

COOPERATIVE PLAY CAR RELAY

Here's an activity that is fun, challenging, exciting, and a great discussion starter. The activity involves a relay between two or more teams of five to ten members each. Each team is given some type of take-apart, put-together toy like Playskool's No. 483 (45-piece toy car). Each team member is to place one piece to the toy. The teams are placed ten to twenty feet from the toy, run up, put their piece on, run back, then the next one comes up, and so on. Before the race begins the captain has a few minutes to inspect the materials and pieces, and plan how to lay them out. Strategy is all important. The captain may give instructions to each team member when they come up to the table, but the captain may not touch or help the team member. Offer a reward to increase the level of competition.

Following the running of the activity and the giving of the reward process, evaluate what happened. Use discussion questions like: Did you want to win? Why? Did anyone cheat? Why? Did they try to help each other? What about the captain? Did the losers blame the captain? Who was responsible for the loss?

This activity may seem juvenile, but the fact is it usually turns into a meaningful discussion and the kids really enjoy the activity involved.

EUTHANASIA ON TRIAL

This mock trial idea not only raises a timely and difficult issue but also allows the entire youth group to participate in the decision-making process.

The setting is a trial or hearing on the issue of euthanasia (this could also work with any other controversial issue). Part of the youth group is designated the jury, the rest are courtroom observers. Youth sponsors can be used as the lawyers to present the pros and cons of the issue to the jury. Youth group members can be chosen to represent family members in the three cases described. The youth minister or another sponsor plays the part of judge. (It is important that the "judge" acquaint himself thoroughly with the issue along with portions of Scripture that are applicable.)

The job of the lawyers is to present a convincing case for either the "pro" or "con" side of the issue using whatever sources they can find to prove their argument. They may also call witnesses (youth group members who represent family members in the cases described) to bolster their case. Of course, there should be opportunity for cross-examination. After both cases have been presented and summary statements made, the jury adjourns for a matter of minutes to vote on the issues. The jury is *not* deciding on the pro and con of euthanasia, rather on Cases A, B, and C. The jury should then vote on each case and give the results to the judge, who will read the results to the "courtroom." (There should be little or no discussion by the jury while deliberating. Save that for the discussion with the whole group later.)

The entire group then discusses the decisions. The judge can wrap up the discussion with some biblical insights without telling the group what they should have concluded. Let the young people go home and struggle with their decision themselves.

Cases for the Jury to Consider

A. Hortense is a severely retarded, nineteen-year-old girl. She has control of her motor (muscle) faculties but seems to be about the age of one or two mentally. After nearly eight years of therapy, doctors and aides have taught her to button the buttons on her clothes. The method they used was much like the method a dog trainer would use to teach a dog tricks: stimulus-response. She might be able to be trained to hold down some extremely simple job on a factory production line, but it would take years to train her. Those years would take large amounts of money both from taxpayers and family. In addition it would take precious time from a doctor or psychiatrist who could be spending his time on someone who was more "promising." The family has asked that they be released from any legal responsibility for Hortense, or if that is not possible, that she be mercifully put to death. The jury must decide.

B. Alex is a successful 47-year-old businessman. He went in to the doctor for a routine check-up and the doctor found a large lump in the middle of Alex's back that he didn't like the looks of. X-rays were taken and it was found to be cancer of some sort. A biopsy was done and the cancer was determined to be malignant. It was too far along to remove so radiation therapy was performed. That was unsuccessful and a month later Alex is in the hospital in a coma. Doctors believe that he won't live more than six months, but he could be given medication (morphine) to lessen the pain. He would have to remain in the Intensive Care Ward till death ($120/day), plus the family would have to bear the cost of doctors' bills and medication totaling thousands of dollars. This family could bear the expense but they cannot bear to see the pain that Alex is in, and so they ask the doctors to either (1) give Alex a lethal dose of morphine or (2) discontinue all medications and care and let him die naturally and hopefully quickly. The jury must decide.

60

C. A baby is born to John and Jane Doe. They have waited for a child for some time, and they both eagerly await the time when they can go on home with their new arrival. The shape of the baby's head bothered a couple of the doctors and routine tests were run to test the baby's brain waves. It was found that during delivery the baby's skull contracted too tightly around the brain and the child suffered severe brain damage to the point that he will be totally mentally deficient. The baby remained in intensive care while John and Jane went home to think the whole matter over. They are just a young couple and have no way financially of putting the child in an institution. They decided to go to the doctor and ask if the child could be put out of his misery, and they would try to have another child. It was brought before the courts and the jury must decide.

Lawyer's Case Against Euthanasia

1. Euthanasia could easily be misconstrued as a mere recommendation of suicide or of wholesale murder of aged or infirmed people.
2. How could a weak and/or unbalanced mind, incapable of weighing aright the conditions which may be held to render death more desirable than life, make this momentous decision?

   Case in point: One miraculous cure given a great deal of publicity was that of a clergyman's wife who, in a widely circulated letter, had begged for "scientific kindness" by her physicians to terminate her suffering and give her painless death. Many laymen supported her arguments, but the physicians ignored them and succeeded in restoring her health. She rejoiced that her pleas were disregarded.

3. What about the obstacles concerning practical applications in our modern society: "Who will determine who is to die and how?
4. If infants born with idiocy, retardation, or complete body disfigurement are put to death under a euthanasia law, this would lead to a degrading of morality, a new form of infanticide, in other words, belated abortion.
5. One alternative is segregation and special training instead of euthanasia. For example, the feeble-minded can be made actually useful, as many of them have considerable physical skill, and they seem to be happy under such conditions.
6. We should hold on to the value of the individual and of life at any cost.
7. Wouldn't a pro-euthanasia morality have a hard time dealing with incidences or mistakes and/or abuse?
8. What about the danger that legal machinery initially designed to kill those who are a pain to themselves may some day engulf those who are a pain to others?

Lawyer's Case for Euthanasia

1. What type of life would a baby have who was born mongoloid or a complete vegetable? The issue is "quality" of life, rather than "quantity."
2. Special segregation and training involves heavy expense of all sorts: emotional and economic.

3. A "carefully controlled system" of euthanasia would eliminate the most hopeless cases at once.
4. The quality of life of those around the incapacitated individual will be adversely affected if the individual is left to linger in pain.
5. There are those who are afflicted with incurable and painful diseases who want to die quickly. A law which tries to prevent such sufferers from achieving this quick death, and thereby forces other people who care for them to watch their pointless pain helplessly, is a very cruel law! In such cases the sufferer may be reduced to an obscene image of a human being, a lump of suffering flesh eased only by intervals of drugged stupor.
6. There should be a concern for human dignity, an unwillingness to let the animal pain disintegrate a person.
7. Suffering is evil. If it were not, why then do we expend so much energy in trying to relieve it?
8. The goal of the euthanasia society "would permit an adult person of sound mind, whose life is ending with much suffering, to choose between an easy death and a hard one, and to obtain medical aid in implementing that choice."

EXCUSES

If you've had trouble recruiting leadership in your church, here is a creative and fun way to get people thinking. "Excuses" is a singing-commercial type of skit with a message that can be presented by your youth to the adults.

Cast: Chairman of nominating committee
Nervous Nell
Hypochondriac Herman
Society Sue
Tired Timothy
Sunday School Superintendent
Tardy Tilly
Hostess Hortense
Last-minute Melvin

Props: (All wear signs stating their "names")
Nervous Nell: large handkerchief
Hypochondriac Herman: hot water bottle, large bottle of pills or a thermometer
Society Sue: gaudy hat, jewelry, fur, lorgnette
Tired Timothy: makeup of "tired lines"
Tardy Tilly: hair curlers, furry slippers, coat
Hostess Hortense: apron, cooking spoon
Last-minute Melvin: bathrobe
Poster, telephone, cardboard letters

SCENE 1

All: (*Sing in unison to the tune of "A Tisket, A Tasket"*)
Excuses, excuses, we always get excuses,
When we ask some folks to help,
We always get excuses!

(*Each member sings one line and holds up corresponding cardboard letter. Song is sung to tune of "Rock-a-Bye, Baby"*)

E-mbarrased to try it,
X-cuse me this year,
C-hildren upset me,
U-lcers, my dear,
S-imply too nervous,
E-xhausted you see,
S-ad nominating committee!

Chairman: (*Sings to tune of "Ten Little Indians"*)
One little, two little, three little excuses,
Everyone is blowing their fuses,
Putting their talents to other uses,
On a Sunday morning.

Nell: (*Enters shaking, biting nails, and wringing hankie; sings to tune of "She'll Be Coming 'Round the Mountain"*)
I just can't teach a class when I come.
I get so nervous, and my legs get numb,
Then if I were prepared,
Then I wouldn't be so scared,
But those children always make me feel so dumb!

Herman: (*Enters carrying hot water bottle in one hand and large bottle of pills, or thermometer, in other hand; sings to tune of "Old Black Joe"*)
Gone are the days when my heart was young and gay.
My health's so bad, may not live out the day.
Don't count on me, I hate to make you sad.
I know you need a teacher, but I feel too *bad!*

Sue: (*Enters peering condescendingly through lorgnette at audience; sings in high falsetto with rolled r's to tune of "Jingle Bells"*)
Every day, PTA,
Brownies or the troop,
I am just so busy now,
My calendar is pooped.
Can't take a class, so I'll pass,
Ask another time.
Maybe I can work it in,
In 1989!

63

Tim: (*Enters with slumped shoulders, slow gait, and sighs loudly before singing to tune of "I've Been Workin' on the Railroad"*)
I have been a superintendent
For the past ten years,
Through the joys and through the sorrows,
The laughter and the tears.
Now my bones are getting weary,
I just can't work so hard.
Get a younger man to do it,
'Cause I am just too 'tard'!

SCENE 2

Scene opens with pianist playing "Reveille" and poster displayed. It says, "Later on Sunday mornings we hear . . ."

Superintendent: (*Pacing back and forth, looking at his watch, sings to tune of "Where Has My Little Dog Gone?"*)
Oh where, oh where, can the teachers be,
Oh why, oh why, aren't they here?
It's a quarter to ten and they haven't come in,
Oh why did they not appear?

Tilly: (*Runs in breathless with coat on only one arm; sings to tune of "Old McDonald Had a Farm"*)
I forgot my teacher's book,
E-I-E-I-O.
I left it on the breakfast nook,
E-I-E-I-O.
With a rush-rush here,
And a rush-rush there,
Brush my teeth and comb my hair,
And couldn't find a thing to wear,
E-I-E-I-O!

Superintendent: (*Still pacing and looking at watch, glances at phone; sings to tune of "Are You Sleeping?"*)
Are they swimming, hedges trimming,
Did they call, did they call?
Picnicking or snoring, they are still ignoring
Their duty, their duty.

Hortense: (*Enters and dials phone; sings to tune of "Reuben, Reuben"*)
I won't be at church this morning.
I would like to, but I can't,
In just walked my father, mother,
Brother, sister, uncle, aunt.
I would like to bring them with me,
But their visits are so rare,
I must give them all my free time,
So I guess I won't be there.

Melvin:	*(Enters in bathrobe, hair disheveled, dials phone, sings to tune of "Farmer in the Dell")* Herman lost his shoe. Matilda drank the glue. Little Fred is still in bed. We think he's got the flu!
All:	*(Sing to the tune of "Oh Susanna")* Now everyone has sung his song, And we must bid adieu, But we are hoping that we brought A little laugh or two. You've seen excuses In jest, but still they're true. Now aren't you glad that you are here, So we can't sing about you!

FACE TO FACE

This game is great for giving people a nonthreatening way to communicate what they believe. It is also great for helping people discover how well they know each other. The game is played by two, three, or four people with a regular deck of playing cards. Each player receives cards of the same suit, except the jack. Jacks and jokers are not used. The players sit face to face and the first player says a sentence expressing an attitude about something. These statements may describe *emotions,* for example, "I feel fine when I am alone"; *opinions* such as, "I am against capital punishment"; *reactions* such as, "I blush when someone praises me"; *tastes* or *preferences* such as, "I like working out of doors"; *values* such as, "I feel it's more important to have a good reputation than to be rich"; or *beliefs* such as, "I believe in reincarnation." Each player indicates his position on the statement made by choosing a card between one (the ace) and ten. He or she chooses the card from one to ten on this basis:

> 1 indicates: total disagreement
> 2 or 3 indicates: strong disagreement
> 4 or 5 indicates: slight disagreement
> 6 or 7 indicates: slight agreement
> 8 or 9 indicates: strong agreement
> 10 indicates: total agreement

The players then place the cards they have chosen face down to their left. For the same statement each player chooses a card which corresponds to the position he or she thinks the other player has chosen. The player places this second card face down to his/her right. The other player does the same thing: he/she places the "me" card to the left and the "you" card to the right. The players then turn over the cards, taking care not to reverse their positions.

Each player counts his points by noting the difference between the value of the right-hand card (the one by which he describes his partner's position) and the card his/her partner has placed before this card, namely his partner's left-hand card. For example, let's say John and Louise are playing Face to Face: John places a 9 to his right, thinking that Louise strongly agrees with the statement just made. Louise, however, has rated her own position with a 5. John's score is 4. Meanwhile, Louise has placed an 8 on her right to indicate what, in her estimation is John's position on the statement. John has rated himself with a 7. So the score for Louise is 1.

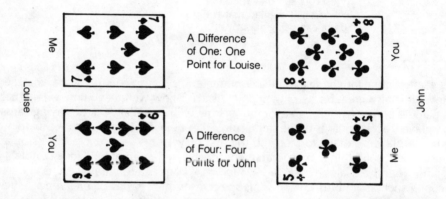

A Difference of One: One Point for Louise.

A Difference of Four: Four Points for John

The players note their scores, take back their cards, and the next player makes a statement. Once again, each player lays down two cards as described above. Points are counted again and the first person or couple to obtain a score of 50 or 100 points loses the game.

If a player does not want to reveal his/her position on the statement given or to guess the position of his or her partner, he/she puts down a king or queen. The score for the player is then the highest of all other scores on the table for that particular round.

NOTE: If there are three players: one person makes a statement and the two others play Face to Face, placing their cards and noting their scores. Then the next person makes a statement and the other two play Face to Face, etc. If there are four players: the two people playing Face to Face add up their points. This couple plays "against" the other couple.

GOD AND THE I.R.S.

Here's a short skit that can generate some good discussion on the effectiveness of prayer. For best results, the actors should memorize their lines and perhaps insert recognizable names and places to make the situation more "local." Four people are needed. The scene: A college fraternity house.

SCENE ONE

Jim: Hi, Mike. What's the matter? You look a little "down."

Mike: Oh, hi, Jim. Yeah, I'm down all right. Tomorrow's the deadline for paying my tuition and I'm just not gonna be able to come up with the cash. So . . . school's out for me, I guess. It's back to the salt mines. . . .

Jim: Gee, that's a shame. What about your folks? Can they help?

Mike: No, not really. My dad's been out of work for the last couple of months, and they are gonna need whatever cash they have just to live on.

Jim: Can you get a loan from somewhere?

Mike: I've already tried. No luck. My credit's no good; my dad's credit's no good; and I still haven't paid off the last loan I managed to con the bank out of.

Jim: How much do you need?

Mike: $750. Cash, check, or money order.

Jim: Wow. That's a lot of dough.

(Enter Bob)

Bob: Hi, guys. What's new?

Mike: 750 bucks. That's what's new.

Bob: Huh?

Jim: He means if he doesn't come up with 750 bucks by tomorrow, it's back to washing dishes at Mabel's.

Bob: Sorry to hear about it, Mike. Lucky for me, my old man has plenty of money. He just writes the school a check every year—no sweat.

Jim: Yeah, me too. Thank God for dads.

Mike: Well, that's great for you, but what about me? What am I gonna do?

Bob: Have you had much experience robbing banks?

Jim: *(laughs)* I hear there's big money in pushing drugs these days.

Mike: Come on, knock it off. This is serious. *(Enter Pete)* Hey, Peter, you got 750 bucks you wanna get rid of?

Pete: Hi, Mike. Hi, guys. 750 bucks? What are you talking about? I couldn't afford a ticket to a free lunch.

Bob: Mike needs money for school by tomorrow or his education comes to a screeching halt.

Pete: A classic case of mal-tuition.

Mike:	Very funny. Ha ha. (*sarcastically*)
Pete:	I suppose you've already discussed trying to get a loan and so on.
Jim:	No good.
Pete:	Have you prayed about it?
Mike:	What? Get serious.
Pete:	I *am* serious. Have you prayed about it?
Bob:	Come on, man. What is God gonna do? Drop 750 dollars out of the sky by tomorrow?
Pete:	How should I know what God will do? But we *are* Christians, aren't we? We *are* supposed to have faith, you know.
Mike:	I think robbing a bank is easier.
Jim:	Look, Mike—it's worth a try. Jesus did say, "Ask and you will receive," didn't He?
Mike:	But I'm not very good at praying. Especially when I'm depressed.
Bob:	Pete, why don't you pray? It was your idea.
Pete:	Okay by me. Let's pray right here. (All four bow their heads, and Pete leads them in a prayer, which he can make up, asking God to help them solve Mike's money problems.)
Mike:	Thanks, Pete. Well, look . . . I better get going and see if I can find a money tree somewhere.
All:	See you later. Good luck, Mike. Hope you find that tree.

SCENE TWO

(Have someone hold up a card to that effect)
(Jim, Bob, and Mike meet again)

Jim:	Hey, Mike! You're looking a little better than you did yesterday. You must have found that money tree.
Mike:	Hey, you're not going to believe what happened.
Bob:	Good news, I hope.
Mike:	After I left you guys yesterday, I went over to my folks' house, and there was an envelope addressed to me from the Internal Revenue Service. Inside it was a check for $774.13. I made a mistake on my taxes last year, they discovered it and refunded my money! What a stroke of luck! I just couldn't believe it!
Jim:	Wow . . . God sure answered that prayer in a hurry!
Mike:	God, nothing, man. It was the I.R.S.! That check was in the mail way before Pete ever prayed. Thank you, Uncle Sam!

GOSPEL ACCORDING TO ME

Pass around sheets of paper or cards with the words printed at the top THE GOSPEL ACCORDING TO _____ . Have them fill in their names and write their own versions of the story of Jesus. They should include their own beliefs about Jesus, including areas where they have doubts. Their "gospels" can be as long or as short as they want them to be.

HOW TO GET TO HEAVEN

Many young people get bogged down with theological terms such as justification, redemption, atonement, sanctification, and so on. Here's a game that helps kids understand the meaning of forgiveness, faith, and grace. Announce that the object of the game is to get enough points to get to heaven. In order to get to heaven, you must have a total of 1000 points. Points are awarded or deducted according to things you have or have not done (see sample list below). Divide the entire group into small groups of four or five each and pass out the list, which shows how to get points. Each group then has 15 minutes to see how many points they can come up with. They can combine points (within the small groups) to try to get a total of 1000, but in that case, only one person can go to heaven for each 1000 points accumulated. Choosing who gets to go is a good source of discussion all by itself.

How to get points:

1 point items:	Good deed done during the past week
	Books of the Bible memorized (in order)
	Each commandment memorized
5 points each:	Each dollar given to the church or the poor during the past week
	Each time you prayed during the past week
	Each time you read the Bible during the past week
	Each church service attended during the past month
10 bonus points:	Bringing a friend (non-member) with you to church
50 bonus points:	Knowing at least three Bible verses (with reference)
	Memorizing one creed (i.e., Apostle's Creed, etc.)
100 bonus points:	Sharing Christ with someone during the past week
	Participating in a service project of some kind during past month (helping the poor, needy, etc.)

Points are deducted for the following:

Minus 1 point for:	Each occasion of swearing during the week
	Each commandment broken this week (see Matt. 5)
	Disobeying parents this week
Minus 5 points for:	Cheating on a test this past month
	Each day you didn't pray this week
	Missing Sunday school this month (per Sunday)
Minus 10 points for:	Each lie told this week
	Every occasion of gossip
	Each day you fail to read your Bible

Of course, you can make up your own lists, depending on the emphasis you'd like the game to have. You can add some, subtract others, or change the value of the items. Stress the importance of honesty while kids are computing their point totals. Try to structure your point system so that the kids can at least get a few points and not end up with a minus score. This phase of the game ends by having the groups announce who (if anyone) gets to go to heaven, and perhaps how they were able to come up with the points.

The game then continues with a search for hope. Most of the kids will realize that, according to the rules of the game (which cannot be changed), they have little hope. What they need is points—lots of them. After sufficient discouragement has set in, announce that you are going to give everyone 1000 free points if they would like them and would take them. After all, it's your game and you can give points if you want to. It doesn't take long for kids to see how God has done the same thing for us. That's what grace is (the free gift of God through His Son, Jesus). All we have to do is accept it through faith in Him.

HYPO'S VS. CHUNS

Here's a creative approach to understanding Matthew 6:1–18. In this passage, Jesus makes a clear distinction between the behavior of the hypocrites ("Hypo's") and the behavior of the Christians ("Chuns"). There are three basic categories referred to:

1. Acts of righteousness (vv. 1–4)
2. Prayer (vv. 5–15)
3. Fasting (vv. 16–18)

Divide your youth group into "Hypo's and "Chuns". Then have each group give an example of each of the categories listed above. You can approach this from a couple of different directions. One approach would be to have the first group ("Hypo's," for example) give an illustration of how they would behave according to category one. You would then have the second group (the "Chuns") use the same illustration but change it to fit their identity. Another approach would be to have each group come up with their own illustration of each category and compare notes after they're finished.

IF YOU WERE TO DIE

The following exercises can be used together or separately to discuss the subject of death and dying.

1. In your opinion, what is the least desirable way to die?
2. If you were to die at 11:00 P.M. tonight, who would you most want to see before you die? Choose two:

Parents	A friend
Brother	Your pastor
A teacher	The coach
A neighbor	A child
Sister	Enemy
Grandparents	

Discuss your answers and the reasons why you answered the way you did.
3. A Situational Exercise:

You are riding down the street in a car and suddenly another car, which is making a left turn, cuts in front of you and smashes into your car. Your car hits the car in the lane next to you and ends up hitting a light pole. You are rushed to the hospital by ambulance where they find out you have a fractured skull, several broken ribs, a cracked collarbone, a broken arm, and broken leg. Needless to say, you are in bad shape and your condition gets worse every hour. You fear that you will soon die, and because you are young you have written no will, so you decide to write one.

Write a will on a separate sheet of paper. Write down personal possessions and whom you would leave them to. Sample line:

I _____ being of sound mind do hereby bequeath the following possessions to the persons named below.

Take some time to discuss how you felt about writing your will and why you chose to leave certain things to certain people.

As the days go by your condition gets worse. Many things are tried to help you recover—special treatment, surgery by specialists—but all to no avail, and finally you pass away. As is customary when someone dies, an obituary appears in the newspaper. Spend several minutes writing your own obituary and thinking about what will be said about you after you die. (Leader may want to read an obituary from a newspaper so the kids get the idea.)

Take some time to review and talk over your feelings about writing your own obituary and what you think will be said about you after your death.

IMAGE OF CHRIST

Here's a short discussion-starter on the person of Jesus Christ. Divide the kids into small groups and give each group one of the Scripture references below to discuss. Then have each group come up with the scriptural "image of Christ" that was in their selection. Have one person in each group present the image discovered in their findings.

Scripture	Image
Philippians 2:5–11	Lord and Servant
Matthew 25:34–40	King and Friend
Isaiah 42:1–9	Suffering Servant
John 10:11–16	Shepherd
John 6:44–51	Teacher and bringer of life
Luke 4:38–44	Compassionate Healer
Matthew 16:13–20	Peter's confession

LIFE AUCTION

Divide your group into small groups and give each group a sheet like the one below. After each group finishes their sheet, bidding begins. After the auction is over, the whole group discusses and evaluates what happened. The items below could be changed and adapted to fit your particular group.

LIFE AUCTION

You have received $5,000 and can spend the money any way you desire. Budget the money in the column labeled "Amount Budgeted." We will then bid on each item in an auction manner. It is your goal to gain the things you most desire.

	AMOUNT BUDGETED	AMOUNT SPENT	HIGHEST BID
1. A wonderful family life without any hassles.			
2. All the money I need to be happy.			
3. Never to be sick.			
4. To find the right mate, who is good-looking and fulfills me.			
5. Never to have pimples.			
6. To be able to do whatever I want whenever I want.			
7. To have all the power the President has.			
8. To be the best-looking person.			
9. To have a real hunger to read the Bible.			
10. To be able to understand all things.			
11. To eliminate all hunger and disease in the world.			
12. To always be close to God.			
13. Never to feel lonely or put down.			
14. Always be happy and peaceful.			
15. Never feel hurt.			
16. To own a beautiful home, car, boat, plane, and seven motorcycles, one for each day of the week.			
17. To be super-smart without ever having to attend school.			
18. To be able to excel in all things.			
19. To be filled with God's presence in the most dynamic way.			
20. To always know that I am in God's will.			
21. To be the greatest athlete in the world.			
22. To be looked up to by everyone else.			
23. To become a TV star.			
24. To always have a lot of close friends.			
25. To walk close to God.			

LONG-DISTANCE ROLE PLAY

Here's an interesting role play using simulated telephone conversations. Give each person a card with one of the following situations written on it. He/she must act out only one side of the conversation, and the rest of the group then tries to guess what is going on.

1. You have just called heaven to complain about the way things are going, and after you have listed all your complaints you find you were talking to God personally.

2. God has just called you to suggest that you break up with your boyfriend/girl friend and you are trying to convince Him otherwise.
3. God has just called to explain that He wants you to be a missionary. You don't really want to be a missionary so you're trying to convince Him that you do, but not right now.
4. God called and wants you to give an account of how you have spent the last three days.
5. You have just experienced a personal tragedy and you call God to ask why it had to happen. He answers the phone, listens to what you have to say, and then hangs up without a word.

THE LORD IS MY SKI BOAT

Putting a biblical passage into contemporary imagery often helps young people understand more clearly the implications of that passage. Try dividing your youth into small groups and, after reading through the twenty-third Psalm, have each group decide on a metaphor and then rewrite this psalm using their metaphor. You can also give the young people a list of metaphors ahead of time and have them form groups around the ones they like. Some options could be: The Lord is my dirt bike; The Lord is my skateboard; The Lord is my math teacher; etc. Here is a sample Psalm 23 rewrite done by a group of junior-high young people:

> The Lord is my ski boat,
> That's just what I've always wanted.
> He makes me ski on blue water;
> He leads me along quiet seas.
> He gives back my zeal for life.
> He guided me behind the wake
> For my well being's sake.
>
> Even though I come to choppy waters,
> I show no fear, for someone is watching.
> Your life jacket and boots, they comfort me.
> You let me jump the wake before my critics and I do not fall.
> My skills are mounting.
> Certainly exciting and successful times will follow me all the days of my life,
> And I will dwell in the skiers Hall of Fame forever.

You may not end up with the greatest theology in the world, but the kids will probably have a lot better grasp of a particular Bible verse than they did before they started.

LOTTERY MEAL

The Lottery Meal can be held as part of a regular youth supper, or, even better, as part of a weekend retreat. Either way, this semi-simulation game can help your youth better understand the frustrations of being poor in a rich society. In order for this to be effective, do not let the young people know that anything unusual will be happening at the dinner. Let them discover the lottery when they show up to eat.

Place play money in plain white sealed envelopes in amounts ranging from $2500 to $50. (10–15 percent of the envelopes contain $2500–the wealthy; 50 percent contain amounts from $1500 to $500–middle-class; 35–40 percent contain amounts from $300 to $50–the poor).

Place the envelopes in a box and have each person draw one envelope to use for purchasing his/her meal at the buffet dinner. In plain view near the buffet table should be a large menu and price list, such as:

Milk—$10	Steak—$1500
Soda—$50	Hamburgers—$100 each
Cake—$300 a piece	Plain spaghetti—$40
Cupcake—$75	Salad—$250

Interaction will vary with each group during serving of the meal, but some reactions to watch for on the part of the have-nots might include those who balk and refuse to ask for more money and those who will go to any extreme to get more money. And on the part of the wealthy you might observe those who make the have-nots grovel for extra cash and those who freely share their money. You might even find the wealthy pooling their money and forming a bank. The discussion possibilities are endless and you will have no trouble getting people to talk. Oh yes, after the discussion, you should arrange for everyone, rich and poor, to serve themselves to a full supper.

OBSTACLE ILLUSION

Here's an activity that is not only fun but has great discussion potential. It's a combination trust-walk and obstacle course. First of all, you'll need a large area with a lot of minor obstacles such as light poles, trees, playground equipment, etc. (One group used the church boiler room after they had shut down all of the heating and cooling equipment.) Then pick a starting point and run some heavy cord to the nearest obstacle. At that point string out two or more lines to other nearby obstacles. Only one line will continue beyond one of the obstacles, the others will dead-end. Continue the main line to the next obstacle with more dead-ends, etc. Mark the end of the course by hanging a coffee can full of marbles from the last obstacle.

Divide into groups of eight to twelve kids. Have each group choose a leader and two or three assistants. Line the kids up in a hand-on-shoulder, single-file line and blindfold each one (unless you are in a room that can be made absolutely dark). Lead each group separately by a confusing path to the starting point and let each group follow the course alone.

Explain to the groups that the object is to follow the main line without separating. (The leader can stop the group while he/she sends out assistants to check when they come to more than one line.)

Note: Be sure to vary the heights of the line. For example, if the main line leads to an obstacle at shoulder level, it could go out from the obstacle at knee or ankle level while a dead-end continues from shoulder level. Also plan obstacles that require the kids to stoop under. Make sure the course is long enough so that it takes twenty to twenty-five minutes to finish!

PAUL'S LETTER TO THE AMERICANS

This is an activity that causes both the kids and leader to reflect on their present lives and help them get a feeling for Paul's letters to the churches.

Have the kids write letters to themselves from "Paul," praising (it's important to praise as well as admonish) and admonishing themselves on their lifestyles. Give them about twenty minutes to write their letters, then break into small groups and have them share their letters.

Another adaptation is to use a specific passage (Eph. 6:10–24, for example) and rewrite it to themselves. Or have small groups compose a letter to the whole youth group, evaluating what the youth group is or is not doing.

PERSONALITY PIT

This game can help your youth group get better acquainted. First, have each person list one thing about himself in each of the following categories:

Age	Career aspirations
Year in school	Favorite summer activity
Height	Favorite sport
Hobby	Name

Then have someone print on blank playing cards (available through many educational materials publishers) one category and response. Make sure the cards represent all of the answers given by your group.

Then shuffle and deal out the cards. The object of the game is to assemble one personality (all seven traits) by trading cards with others. Any number of cards can be traded at one time, but must be exchanged for the same number of cards in return (just like the commercial game of Pit). Play continues until someone collects all the cards which they believe describes one person in the group. The person whose personality was being described is then given a chance to confirm or deny the information.

PICTURING FORGIVENESS

Have the kids in your group look up the following Bible passages and list from them as many "word pictures" about how God forgives our sins as possible. Most groups ought to be able to come up with five or six. The passages are: Psalm 103:11–12; Isaiah 38:17; 43:25; and Micah 7:18–19. These word pictures might include someone being pulled from a well, throwing sins behind your back, blotting out or wiping away sins (off a blackboard perhaps), and so on.

After the kids have done this, have them choose the one that seems to mean the most to them personally. Give them some marking pens and paper or other art supplies, and have them actually draw, paint, make a collage, or use any other method to graphically present their forgiveness word picture. When these are completed, allow each person to share the meaning of his or her picture with the rest of the group.

Finally, spend about five minutes with the entire group brainstorming a completely unique word picture for forgiveness, not one found in Scripture. You might want to make it very contemporary or abstract. This can also be graphically pictured, perhaps as a large mural to hang on the wall of the meeting room or elsewhere in the church.

RIGHT AND WRONG

Display a poster like the one illustrated below before the entire group. Remove it after all have read it to themselves. They should not discuss it yet. Then pass out pencils and paper and have them write out the phrase they just saw. Chances are good that most of the kids will be wrong. Most people don't notice that the word *A* is included twice.

Follow up with a discussion on how easy it is to be mistaken about something, even when you are sure you are right. Focus particularly on how we see only what we want to see, how we tend to go along with the majority—even when it is possible that they may be wrong, how we often make decisions based on preconceived ideas or on wrong information, etc. Discuss ways that will help us to make right decisions and to determine right from wrong.

ROLE BOWL

Print up the following situations on cards and put them in a bowl. Let each person in a small group pick one out and think about it. Ask the kids to share their solutions to the situation. (Of course, the more verbal kids will share first. But don't *force* anyone to share!) After each person finishes, allow others in the group to comment or add their own thoughts.

1. I don't get it. If Christianity is true, how come there are so many religions that call themselves Christian? I mean, what's the difference between Baptists, Presbyterians, etc.?
2. If you ask me, the Christian religion makes you a "doormat"—always loving and turning-the-other-cheek stuff.
3. What if I lived recklessly for eighty years and then became a Christian on my deathbed? Would Billy Graham and I go to the same place?
4. I've been reading through the Old Testament for English class. How come God ordered His people to kill everybody—even women and children—when they conquered a land? What kind of a God is that?
5. Your mother and I don't believe in all this Jesus stuff and we think you spend too much time in church. So we want you to stay away from church for a while.
6. If God is God, then why can't you see Him? Why don't you prove that God exists? Go ahead . . . prove it to me.
7. The Bible has some nice little stories in it, but everyone knows it's full of contradictions, errors, and just plain myths. How can you believe it?
8. I know a bunch of people who go to your church. They're supposed to be Christians, but I also know what they do during the week and at parties that I go to. They're phonies. If Christianity is so great, why are there so many phonies?
9. My little brother died of leukemia, although I had prayed like crazy. Don't tell me God loves us. How come He didn't help my brother?
10. Look, I know I'm overweight. I started coming to your church because I thought the kids in your youth group would treat me differently than the kids do at school. Wrong! They ignore me and make fun of me just like everyone else. How come?

THE SECRET

Mr. and Mrs. Benjamin are close friends with Bob and Lisa Sanders. Both couples are long-time members of the same church, pastored by Reverend Evans.

All three couples are having dinner at the Benjamins' house Saturday night. A few days before the dinner, while Mrs. Benjamin is out shopping, she notices a commotion at the exit. Apparently, someone is being stopped for shoplifting. To Mrs. Benjamin's amazement, that someone is Lisa Sanders. Shocked and embarrassed, Mrs. Benjamin darts out of the store not knowing whether Lisa saw her or not.

Mrs. Benjamin feels very close to Lisa and plans to discuss the matter privately with her. But she is worried that such a discussion might damage their relationship.

Mr. Benjamin believes it should be forgotten.

Bob Sanders has no idea his wife is shoplifting. The knowledge of such would be humiliating to him, and he would have a difficult time understanding and forgiving.

Lisa Sanders knows that Mrs. Benjamin saw her and wants desperately to get help from her friends but is afraid her husband could not handle it.

Reverend Evans is totally unaware of Lisa Sander's problem.

Mrs. Evans has a difficult time accepting the fact that Christians sin—especially something like shoplifting.

The situation: Just as the three couples sit down for dessert, a teen-age son of the Benjamins runs in, saying loudly, "Hey, mom, Sonny just told me that Mrs. Sanders got arrested for shoplift—" (He suddenly sees Mr. and Mrs. Sanders).

Have those chosen beforehand role-play this situation. When you feel enough has been said, stop the role play and discuss what happened. Ask the role players to discuss what they were feeling and then get comments from the group.

SECRET PEN PALS

Drop this idea to the president of your church's women's organization. That group is always looking for worthwhile projects, and this one is great for breaking down barriers between generations.

Provide a list of all the members of your youth group—complete with names, addresses, and birthdays—to your women's organization. They in turn prepare the names and additional information on slips of paper. The women draw names. Then, throughout the year, each woman provides gifts at Christmas, birthday, and any other desired time to her "Secret Pen Pal" without signing her name. It adds to the excitement if the women leave monthly notes, etc., on the church bulletin board or have them delivered at Sunday school time.

At the end of the year, plan a banquet given by the women's organization in honor of the youth. Each woman provides a ticket for herself, her husband (if she's married), and her Secret Pen Pal. After a fun program, the women reveal their pen pals and draw new names. The young people can be encouraged to bring a gift to present to their pen pal, and during the year the kids can leave notes of appreciation for gifts and letters on the bulletin board as well.

TEN YEARS FROM NOW

Here's a fun discussion-starter for junior highs (and others, for that matter). Print the following on a half sheet of paper and give the kids time to answer. Don't have them put their names on the paper (if your group is shy) and discuss them as a group. If your kids don't mind sharing their responses, then simply go around the group and discuss each one individually.

TEN YEARS FROM NOW

1. My height will be . . .
2. My weight will be . . .
3. My hair style will be . . .
4. I will be living . . .
5. I will be working as a . . .
6. My dreams and goals will be . . .
7. I will have been a success in life if . . .
8. I will look back upon this year as a year of . . .

THANKSGIVING GRAFFITI

Have some young people hang up a large blank sheet of paper in a well-traveled area in your church. The pastor should announce that after the service people are invited to write, print, or draw something that represents what they are thankful for. The young people should be ready with felt-tip pens, crayons, watercolors, etc. for people to use. If this is done early in November, the resulting graffiti can be displayed in a prominent place to remind people of how much we have to be thankful for.

TO MARRY OR NOT TO MARRY

The following questionnaire is very helpful as a discussion-starter on the subject of marriage. Print it up and give the group enough time to think through their answers. Then discuss each question and try to come up with a group consensus. Encourage each person to answer the question honestly, as they think they should be answered, rather than answering them the way the church, parents, or tradition would want them to answer.

1. I think everyone ought to get married.

   Definitely YES   Definitely NO
   _____

   (Put an "x" somewhere on the continuum.)

2. If a person decides to opt for marriage, I think the best age for marriage would be: (Circle the best answer.)

   Girls—16 17 18 19 20 21 22 23 24 25 26 27 28 29 30 Over 30

   Boys—16 17 18 19 20 21 22 23 24 25 26 27 28 29 30 Over 30

3. When you are married, are you considered an adult, regardless of age?

YES   NO

(Circle one.)

4. What do you think of the following statement: "God has made one special person in the world for you to marry"?

STRONGLY AGREE   STRONGLY DISAGREE

_____

(Put an "x" somewhere on the continuum.)

5. Marriage is—

a legal statement._____
a social custom._____
God-ordained._____
a religious ceremony._____
a parent-pleaser._____

(Rank these from 1 to 5.)

6. Most people get married because—

they have to._____
they want to have kids._____
they love each other._____
tax benefits _____
they want to have sex legally._____

(Rank these from 1 to 5.)

7. Our concept of marriage is most influenced by—

friends._____   church._____
television._____   books._____
movies._____   celebrities._____
other adults._____   tradition._____
parents._____

(Pick the top three.)

8. What are my top priorities in marriage?

Children_____   Finances_____
Sex_____   Security_____
Communication_____   In-law relationships_____
Mutual trust confidence   Faithfulness_____
   in the other person_____ Romantic love_____
Mutual interests_____

(Rank from 1 to 10.)

9. Divorce is wrong—

always (no exceptions)._____
except when adultery is involved._____
except when both are incompatible._____
except when you don't love each other any more._____

(Check the best answer or answers.)

10. Divorce is—

better than living together when you hate each other._____
a necessary evil._____
a possibility for any one of us._____
a cop-out._____
never okay when children are involved._____
sin._____

(Check the best answer or answers.)

11. Living together (not married) is—

WRONG (always)   OKAY (always)

_____

(Put an "x" somewhere on the continuum.)

12. Living together (not married) is—

better than traditional custom of dating._____
the best way to determine if marriage will last._____
not the same as marriage._____
more acceptable than marriage._____
the best alternative to marriage._____
none of the above._____

(Check best answer or answers.)

TRUTH OR DARE

Pass out two 3 x 5 cards and a pencil to each participant. On one card have them put a question about the Christian life which they would like answered, fold it in half, and mark it with a "T." This card is placed in a box marked "Truth." On the other card they put a "Christian" dare—something they dare someone to do for Christ in the next week (be specific and make it something possible). This card is folded in half, marked with a "D," and put in the "Dare" box.

Now, one participant chooses one card at random from the "Truth" box and tries to answer the question. No one else can speak until he/she has answered. Then discuss whether the others agree or disagree, and why. (The person who answers the question must tell why he/she gave his/her answer.)

After the discussion, the participant draws a card from the box marked "Dare," reads it to the group, and keeps the card to remind him/her to do that thing for Christ that week. Proceed until each person has had a chance to answer a "Truth" question and chosen a "Dare" card. You can usually handle between six and ten questions in an hour, depending on how much discussion is allowed. For larger groups, divide into small groups of five or six.

"Truth or Dare" has been used successfully with high school youth. It lets you know what the kids are thinking; it give them a chance to ask questions anonymously; and it challenges them to do something positive that week.

TWENTY-FIVE-CENT MATE

Give each person a copy of the questionnaire below and give them enough time to complete it. Then go around the group and discuss each person's answers and why they answered as they did.

You may spend 25 cents to "buy" a mate. Select all the qualities you wish from the list below, but do not spend over 25 cents. Put the amount you are spending in the column at the right. In the left-hand column, spend 25 cents on yourself, for becoming the kind of person you wish to be.

Each of this group costs 6 cents:

	A good-looking face	_____	_____
	Very popular	_____	_____
	Intelligent	_____	_____
	A great Christian	_____	_____
	Very kind	_____	_____

Each of these costs 5 cents:

	A well-built figure/body	_____	_____
	A good conversationalist	_____	_____
	Tactful and considerate	_____	_____
	Happy and good sense of humor	_____	_____

Each of this group costs 4 cents:

	Large chest or bust	_____	_____
	Athletic	_____	_____
	Attends church—is religious	_____	_____
	Honest—doesn't lie or cheat	_____	_____

Each of this group costs 3 cents:

	Nicely dressed and well-groomed	_____	_____
	Likes drama, art, and music	_____	_____
	Well-mannered—comes from nice home	_____	_____
	Ambitious and hard-working	_____	_____

Each of this group costs 2 cents:

    The right height   ____ ____

    Gets good grades   ____ ____

    Likes children   ____ ____

    Brave—stands up for rights   ____ ____

Each of this group costs 1 cent:

    Choice of color in eyes and hair   ____ ____

    Owns a car   ____ ____

    Wealthy—or moderately so   ____ ____

    Sincere and serious   ____ ____

UN-DINNER FOR WORLD HUNGER

This is a good meal idea to help your group become aware of the world hunger problem. It could become an annual event. The following menu can be displayed on a buffet with signs indicating price values. It should be explained that everyone may order their choice—13¢ worth of food, representing the daily food budget of many in the world.

MENU

Water — 1¢	Olives — 2¢ each
Coffee — 6¢ a cup	Orange slices — 8¢ each
Sugar — 2¢	Hard-boiled eggs — 6¢ each
Milk — 2¢	Carrots — 3¢ a serving
Saltines — 1¢ each	Sweet pickles — 2¢ a serving
American cheese — 6¢	Raisins — 9¢ a serving
Radishes — 1¢ a serving	Cookies — 3¢ each

Of course, the meal should be followed by a discussion of the problems of world hunger and one's own personal involvement. The price of a regular dinner can be charged as admission, and the difference between it and the un-dinner can be given to Bread for the Word or World Vision for distribution.

UNFAIR

The following is a role play (or socio-drama) that involves five people. The background can be given to the total group, but the instructions should be given to the characters only. Follow up with a discussion on the issues that are raised. For help in coming up with more questions for discussion, see the chapter in this book entitled "Case Studies."

Characters:

Boy 1, girl 1, Frank (brothers and sister); boy 2 and girl 2 (brother and sister). Frank is a freshman in college; the other four are in high school.

Background:

The five of you have been close friends for about ten years. You grew up in the same neighborhood, living only two houses apart. As your parents were friends, you often spent time at each other's homes, always staying with your friends when your parents went out of town. You were the nucleus of the neighborhood "gang." You walked to and from school together; in high school, when Frank got a car, the five of you always rode together.

You've done just about everything together. When you're with someone that much, you're able to talk to each other pretty well. As best friends, you've shared a lot of problems and hurts with each other. That has made you even closer. Really, the only area that you haven't been together on is the matter of religion. Boy 2 and girl 2 have always gone to the Methodist church and Sunday school every Sunday. Boy 1 and girl 1 never got interested in going to church, though Frank would go every once in a while.

Last fall when Frank came home from college for a weekend, he seemed a little different. When the five of you went out for a pizza, he suddenly started talking about becoming a Christian. He seemed a little embarrassed about the whole thing, and at first you thought he had gone off the deep end and was going to start witnessing or something. But he didn't. He just said that he had become a Christian, that his relationship with God meant a lot to him now, and that he felt that he was a better person for it.

Frank came home about every other weekend, and you really started to notice a change in his behavior. He was easier to get along with; he didn't get angry when boy 1 accidently backed his car into a tree; he seemed to listen more closely to what you said and to care more openly about you. This was strange at first, but you came to like the changed Frank. Sometimes big brothers can be a real pain; Frank was turning out to be a really neat person. When you finally asked him about all this, he just said that he was trying hard to be a Christian, and that with God's help, he felt that he could be different.

Frank was coming home for the holidays on Christmas Eve, as he had to work at his job at school all day. It was a snowy night, and about fifty miles south of home Frank's car was hit by a semi-trailer which jackknifed on the expressway. Frank was killed instantly. You found out later that the truck driver was drunk.

It was a rough time for both of your families. The four of you, especially, felt a deep sense of loss. Somehow you couldn't talk about it the way you used to, maybe it just hurt too much right now. But you still held together as a group; you cared about each other.

Instructions:

(To boy 1 and girl 1) Frank's loss has been especially rough on you. You are emotionally worn out. The hurt will never be gone, but you have learned to live with it. You are angry now. The new Frank was a neat person, and you were almost starting to believe what he was saying about God. But how can God who is supposed to be "love" allow someone to be killed as Frank was? It was the other guy who was drunk! It simply wasn't fair. Frank was young, with a lot to do in his life, and he was a

Christian! What kind of God can let someone like Frank die, and the drunken truck driver live?

Finally in desperation, you have decided to talk to boy 2 and girl 2. They have gone to church for some reason, maybe they understand what is going on. (Take it from there.)

VALUES TEASERS

Here are some values clarification stories that can help your youth group find out what they believe.

The Talking Friend

A good friend of yours and yourself are both equally unprepared for a test, and together you cheat and pass. Your friend, however, begins to feel guilty about it and confesses to the teacher. In the process your friend implicates you as well and you both automatically fail the test.

1. Should the friend have confessed?
2. Couldn't the friend just have confessed to God and not the teacher?
3. Should the friend have told the teacher about you?

The Borrowing Brother

You and your brother share the same bedroom. You have made it very clear to your brother, however, that he is to leave your belongings alone. You have a large record collection and a stereo which you purchased with your own money. You come home from school one day and find many of your best records out collecting dust and your favorite record sitting on the window sill getting warped by the sun. You blow up at your brother. He apologizes and offers to buy a new record, but you're still furious. You threaten to tell your parents about it and refuse to accept his apology. You tell him to get out of your room. Finally he has enough and says to you, "I know that you have been seeing Linda even though mom and dad told you not to. You have been telling the folks that you get off work at ten but you really get off at nine. And if you keep yelling at me and threatening me, I'm going to tell them what I know."

1. What's wrong with not wanting to let others use valuable possessions?
2. Which person in this situation is the worst in your opinion? Why?
3. Is blackmail wrong?

The Changing Parents

One evening a couple of your friends come by and you all decide to attend a movie the next weekend. You ask your parents, and although they have never heard of the movie, they give their permission. The next Friday night your friends come to the house to pick you up and your folks ask where you are going. You remind them that they had given you permission to go to a movie. Your dad responds, "Well, I did some checking, and I was going to talk to you. I forgot you were going tonight. But from what my friends tell me the movie is no good. It contains a lot of profanity and explicit sex, so I don't think you can see it. Sorry, but you can't go." Your friends look at each other with shock and amazement. They can't believe it. Just as they leave, you see them smile at each other like they think your folks are real losers. You are embarrassed, humiliated, and angry.

1. Did the parents do the right thing?
2. Do parents have the right to change their minds at the last minute?
3. If you were a parent, how would you have handled the situation?
4. If your parents would have done this, how would you have responded?

VERBAL PUZZLE

This game can be very effective in illustrating the difficulty of following and understanding oral instructions . . . and it's fun. Choose three to six couples and have the partners sit back to back so they cannot see each other's cut-out designs.

One person of each couple has the puzzle design arranged in complete order. His/her partner has the same puzzle design scrambled. The partner with the completed puzzle describes each piece and where to place it. The couple to finish first wins. Allow all others to finish and then have a group discussion on what they learned about communication through this exercise.

Questions:

1. How did you feel? Confused, frustrated, angry, rushed?
2. What causes us to misunderstand what others say or mean?
3. React to this statement: "What I heard you say is not what you meant."

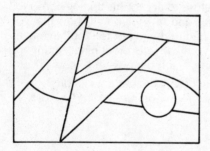 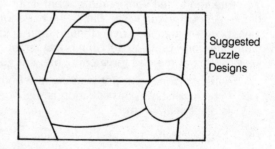

Suggested Puzzle Designs

WHAT DO YOU SAY?

All of us would like to help our young people learn how to develop deep and meaningful relationships with people. But how? Here are some practical exercises that cause young people to think through their responses to people in need and develop interpersonal skills they can use all their lives.

Situation A

A woman is dying of cancer. She is not an active participant in spiritual fellowship, but does attend worship services. She has three children, ages 12–18. You've been visiting her in her hospital room. She has just been sharing some concern about her oldest son who's in some trouble. You've prayed with and for her and are excusing yourself to leave. She begins crying. What do you say and/or do to allow her to express any feelings she may have? Why?

1. "Is there anything you'd like to share with me?"
2. "I see you have some deep feelings. What are you crying about?"
3. "It's really difficult being in the hospital when you're concerned about your children, isn't it?"
4. "I'm sorry. (pause) Good-by." (You exit.)
5. "It's really hard to say good-by, isn't it?"
6. " _____ ."

Situation B

You have a good friend (teen-ager) whose father has just died unexpectedly. The friend has been out of school for several days and has just returned to school. You see this friend in the hall after school. What do you say or do?

1. "I hear your father just died. Gee, that's too bad."
2. "I'm sorry about your dad. But it must be God's will."
3. "Hi! How are ya? (pause) Good to see ya!"
4. "It's hard to lose your dad during your high school years, when you really need his friendship, isn't it?"
5. " _____ ."

Situation C

Your brother or sister has just had a fight with your mom and dad. They forgot to tell your sibling that they had something planned for Saturday and that he/she couldn't do the thing he/she had been planning on doing. Your sibling stomps angrily back to the room you share and begins mumbling and grumbling about how unfair the situation is. You say:

1. "Yeah, isn't the just like parents? I get treated that way, too!"
2. "Let's forget to do the next thing we're supposed to do!"
3. "It's rough, isn't it? It's hard being No. 2."
4. "You feel insignificant and unimportant, don't you?"
5. " _____ ."

Situation D

You're responsible for leading a small group of kids. You know Herbert in your group is extremely shy. You want to encourage Herb to trust the group, be himself, and share his feelings. You decide to share your answer to the discussion question first. After you share, what do you say or do next?

1. "O.K., we're all going to share around the circle, starting with Fred."
2. "O.K., we're all going to share our thoughts. Herb, you first."
3. "Would anyone else like to be the next person to share?"
4. "I think Herb might have some great thoughts. Would you share them with us, Herb? We'd really appreciate it."
5. "_____."

Situation E

You're square dancing with a large group of kids. You're right in the middle of a dance with the other seven members of your set of eight. Suddenly one of the girls, who's been looking "blue" and getting quieter minute by minute, rushes out of the room crying. The music continues but your set has difficulty dancing with only seven people. Finally, the dance ends and a break is called. You move outside to find the girl sitting on the steps. What do you say or do?

1. "What's the matter? What's happened? Why are you crying?"
2. "Hey, you loused up our square of dancers!"
3. You say, "Hi!" softly, then you sit down beside the girl, put your arm around her and don't say anything for several minutes (or until she does).
4. "Growing up is really hard, isn't it?"
5. "Hey, social butterflies don't fly away! Come back inside with me."
6. "_____."

WHAT WOULD YOU DO?

Sometimes it's easier to get into Scripture when it can be looked at in light of some everyday situations. The following six situations are designed to help kids to think through various passages of Scripture and how they might apply them personally. One good way to use them would be to divide the entire group into six small groups and type up each of the situations on separate sheets. Then give each group one of the situations and enough time to work through the discussion questions. When they're finished, each group can then share their conclusions with the other groups.

Jeremiah 17:9–10 (Cheating)

In an English exam you need an A or B to pass the course for the semester. You studied long and hard. You friend didn't study at all. While the teacher is busy checking papers, you notice that your friend is copying answers from another student who always does well. You get a C while your friend gets an A.

1. How do you feel?
2. What would you do as a Christian?
3. Does this experience change your relationship with your friend?
4. Would you discuss the issue with your friend? Other friends? Your parents? The teacher?
5. How would you feel if you were the cheater with an A, knowing your friend studied and received only a C when he needed at least a B?

Proverbs 1:29–31 (Instant Gratification)

The group is going to an amusement park and you need twenty dollars. Your parents agree to help you earn it by allowing you to keep money from the recycling of aluminum cans and the return deposits on soda bottles. Normally that money is put into the family entertainment budget. On the way home with the money, you discover a new album by your favorite rock group and decide you can get the money for the trip from the next returns, so you buy it. When you get home your parents are upset and tell you that they will not help you earn any more money and, because you broke the agreement, you cannot go on the trip even if you have the money.

1. How do you feel?
2. How do you think your parents might feel?
3. Who was cheated?
4. Has an impulsive act such as the above ever cost too high a price?
5. If you were the parent, would you have handled this differently? If so, how?

Proverbs 3:1–6 (Trust)

You're not allowed to go on dates. You've agreed to meet your girl/boyfriend at the movies. You tell your parents you are going to the movies with your best friend. Your parents discover what you did. Now you can go nowhere unless taken and picked up by your parents. Over the last few weeks you feel they are beginning to trust you again.

1. Did you "fess up" or try to "fake it"?
2. Will you sneak again now that they are beginning to trust you again?
3. How do you think your parents felt when you betrayed their trust in you?
4. Would a Christian react differently?

Proverbs 16:6 (Loyalty)

You're at your friend's house. Your friend "sneaks" a candy bar for you. You say nothing even though you think it's not quite right not to ask. On the way home from school you and your friend stop at the store to pick up an item for your mom. When you leave the store your friend gives you a candy bar. After you've eaten it, your friend tells you he/she "sneaked" it for you from the store.

1. How does the candy taste now?
2. How do you feel about your friend?
3. Should you tell someone? Who?
4. Should you have discussed it earlier when you noticed that the friend was "sneaking" the candy at home?
5. Would you discuss this with your parents? Why or why not?
6. If this pattern continues, does your friend deserve your loyalty?
7. Can you get into trouble for being loyal? How or why not?
8. Does loyalty overlook anything and everything?

Deuteronomy 5:16; 1 Samuel 19:1–3 (Obedience)

Your parents do not allow you to call boys on the telephone. You feel times have changed and your parents are old-fashioned. You go to a neighbor's house "to use the phone". The neighbor discovers you're using the phone to call boys and also knows that your parents do not approve or allow it.

1. In what position do you place the neighbor?
2. Do you know why your parents do not want you to phone boys?
3. Do you open discussions with your parents or just complain to your friends?
4. Do you expect parents to automatically know how you feel? Why or why not?
5. Will your parents trust you if they find out?
6. Did you consider the consequences of being found out?

Matthew 25:34–40 (Respect for Others)

Your youth group goes on a retreat. You find yourself in a discussion group. You're not being included so you speak up but the others ignore you. You ask a question or make a suggestion. They pour cold water on your idea. You attempt to sit closer to the nucleus of the group and someone pulls the chair out from under you just as you sit down.

1. How did you feel?
2. Could you have done anything to improve your situation?
3. What should the group have done?
4. Did it upset you that it came from a church group rather than a school group?
5. If you had been part of the antagonizing group, what would or could you have done to improve the situation?
6. Have you ever been part of a group that excluded someone? How did you feel? What were your thoughts? Your actions?
7. Would a Christian react differently?

WISDOM TEST

Here's an interesting discussion-starter on the subject of wisdom based on Proverbs 7–9. Give each of the kids in your group a copy of the following survey; and after they have completed it, discuss each of the questions in depth.

1. My friends and family generally consider me to be . . .
   a. a foolish person.
   b. lacking common sense.
   c. a "wise guy."
   d. able to make fairly wise decisions except when it comes to _____.
   e. wiser than most people.
   f. one of the wisest people in the world.

2. I consider myself to be . . .
   a. a foolish person.
   b. lacking common sense.

    c. a "wise guy."
    d. able to make fairly wise decisions except when it comes to _____.
    e. wiser than most people.
    f. one of the wisest people in the world.

3. I can be talked into things . . .
    a. always or almost always.
    b. often even when I know it is a foolish decision.
    c. only when I really wanted to be in the first place.
    d. sometimes when I see new information.
    e. only when physical violence accompanies the talk.
    f. never.

4. My wisest actions have . . .
    a. resulted in benefits even others can see.
    b. brought about changes only I can appreciate.
    c. are still foolish when compared with the actions of most people.
    d. are just about like everyone else's wisest actions.
    e. are wiser than those of anyone else I know.

5. When I'm criticized, I generally . . .
    a. punch out the person who criticized me.
    b. react by screaming and/or yelling.
    c. pout and try to make the person who criticized me feel guilty.
    d. ignore the criticism.
    e. try to honestly evaluate the criticism and change my ways if I feel it is warranted.
    f. appreciate the person who had the guts to share with me and tell him/her so.

6. One area where I generally show wisdom in my life is . . .
    a. money/finances.
    b. God.
    c. friendships.
    d. sex.
    e. family.
    f. use of time/schedule.
    g. food.
    h. _____.

7. One area where I rarely show wisdom and need drastic improvement is . . .
    a. money/finances.
    b. God.
    c. friendships.
    d. sex.
    e. family.
    f. use of time/schedule.
    g. food.
    h. _____.

YOUTH GROUP CREEDS

Most church bodies have definite stands on social and moral issues such as marriage, sex, pollution, war, homosexuality, divorce, alcohol, tobacco, euthanasia, abortion, other religions, materialism, and so forth. Have your group write up their own creed or statement of belief on one or more of these topics without knowing the "official" position of the church. When they're done, compare their stance with the church's. This can lead into a discussion of the difference or similarity of the creeds, and also about how such creeds are arrived at. Chances are there will be some argument over the youth group creed. They will begin to understand how difficult it is for a whole church to agree on something.

Skits

Skits

DR. PERRIWINKLE, PSYCHIATRIST

Characters: Dr. Albert Perriwinkle, a loud, fast-talking eccentric
The Announcer, a quiet, polite "straight man"
Horris Morris Franklin, a nervous patient
Nurse Comstock

Props: A desk for the doctor. Chairs for the Doctor, Announcer, and Franklin. Paper and scissors. Ink blots.

Announcer: (*in front of curtain*) We are proud to be able to present to you, right now, an interview with world-famous psychiatrist Dr. Albert Perriwinkle. (*Curtain opens. Doctor is seated behind his desk working with paper and scissors.*)

Doctor: (*to himself*) One more cut . . . There! (*reveals paper dolls*)

Announcer: Good evening, Doctor.

Doctor: (*hides dolls*) Who said that?

Announcer: I did, Doctor. Excuse me, over here.

Doctor: There you are! You mustn't do that! You could drive a person nuts doing that. What are you, crazy or something? Oh. Of course you are. That's why you came to me. I'm a doctor (*suddenly not sure*), aren't I? There must be something around here that says I am. (*searches desk*) Ah-ha! Stationery. There must be a name on it. (*reading*) Albert Perriwinkle. Woooo! What a weird name. I've got to get out of here before he catches me.

Announcer: You *are* Dr. Albert Perriwinkle.

Doctor: Are you sure? (*checks the lining of his coat*) Son of a gun, you're right! (*settles back in chair*) Now then, what's your problem?

Announcer: I don't have any problems.

Doctor: False security!

Announcer: No, really. We're just here for an interview.

Doctor: A what?

95

Announcer:	An interview.
Doctor:	Huh?
Announcer:	(*shouts*) An interview!
Doctor:	There's no need to shout. Now sit down over here and tell me about your problem.
Announcer:	Doctor, you don't seem to understand. (*sits down*) I'd like to ask you a few questions.
Doctor:	Why didn't you say that in the first place? Ask away.
Announcer:	When did you first—
Doctor:	Excuse me. That isn't going to be on TV is it?
Announcer:	No, Doctor.
Doctor:	'Cause if it was I'd comb my hair.
Announcer:	It isn't.
Doctor:	Does my hair look all right?
Announcer:	(*fed up*) IT LOOKS FINE! Now, if I may continue. When did you first— (*Enter Nurse Comstock*)
Nurse:	Doctor, Mr. Franklin is here to see you.
Announcer:	Is Mr. Franklin one of your regular patients?
Doctor:	No. This is his first appointment.
Announcer:	May we stay and watch?
Doctor:	It's highly irregular.
Announcer:	We might be able to get it on television.
Doctor:	Sit over in the corner and be very quiet. (*combs hair*) Send Mr. Franklin in, Nurse. (*Exit Nurse Comstock. Enter Mr. Franklin. He sits.*)
Doctor:	Your name, Sir?
Franklin:	Franklin—
Doctor:	Ben Franklin? I've been an admirer of yours for years! I use your electricity all the time! What's your problem?
Franklin:	First of all, I'm not Ben Franklin.
Doctor:	Of course you are.
Franklin:	My name is Horris Morris Franklin.
Doctor:	But you call yourself Ben Franklin.
Franklin:	NO!
Doctor:	It's understandable with a name like Horris Morris. Ha! Ha! Horris Morris!
Franklin:	(*starts to get up*) I don't think—
Doctor:	That's the problem: You don't think. Now sit down, Mr. Franklin. Ben. Tell me about yourself.
Franklin:	Well, I was recommended to you by Dr. Goldblat.

96

Doctor:	Dr. Goldblat? Dr. Goldblat? You've got to be crazy to go to him! Let's look at some ink blots. When you see the ink blots, just tell me the first thing that comes into your mind. Don't feel embarrassed. Whatever you say will be held in the strictest confidence.
Franklin:	But—
Doctor:	Now, I know what you're going to say. You're afraid I'll laugh at what you have to say. Let me put your mind at ease. I'm a doctor. And I'm very serious about my work. Now, what does this ink blot look like to you?
Franklin:	(*apprehensive*) Ah . . . ah . . . an automobile. It looks like an automobile.
Doctor:	An automobile? (*stifles his laughter*) How about this one?
Franklin:	A grasshopper.
Doctor:	(*struggling to keep from laughing*) What's this one?
Franklin:	A piano.
Doctor:	(*bursts out laughing*) Ha ha ha! A piano! That takes the cake! Ha ha! (*walks over to side of stage*) Hey, Hazel! This nut thinks number twelve is a piano! Mr. Announcer, did you hear that one?
Franklin:	(*starting to rise*) I'd better be going.
Doctor:	Don't move. (*regaining his seriousness*) I have discovered your problem.
Franklin:	What is it?
Doctor:	Your instinctual drives lead only to regression, repression, and paranoia in your oral character. Meanwhile, back in your little land of id, your superego is being assaulted by schizophrenia, transference, and all sorts of defense mechanisms.
Franklin:	What does all that mean?
Doctor:	You're a very sick person.
Franklin:	Doctor, do you believe in shock treatments?
Doctor:	Wait till you get my bill. (*Enter Nurse Comstock*)
Nurse:	Doctor, you're scheduled to see Jack Masters now. (*Nurse and Franklin exit.*)
Doctor:	Thank you, Nurse Comstock. (*to Announcer*) I must be going.
Announcer:	Do you have to visit Mr. Masters in the hospital?
Doctor:	No. Mr. Masters thinks he's a dog and I have to walk him.

FASHION FOLLIES

A crazy fashion show always makes a great skit if it's done with a little creativity. The following ideas work great when you set up the stage for a fashion show, with a good announcer who describes the various fashions, and good "fashion models" (boys or girls) who try to walk and wiggle like real models. The results can really be funny. Use these or think of some of your own:

1. *Sack Dress*

   A dress made of a potato sack, with more paper sacks hung all over it—maybe even a sack over the model's head.

2. *Dinner Dress*

   A dress with menus, napkins, salt-and-pepper shakers, plates, food, etc., hanging all over it.

3. *Spring-flowered Dress*

   Dress with real flowers and springs attached to it. Purse can be a bucket with fertilizer, tools, etc.

4. *Tea Dress*

   A dress with tea bags all over it, and a tea pot handbag.

5. *Multi-colored Skirt and Scatter-pin Sweater*

   A skirt with crayons and coloring book pictures all over it; the sweater has dozens of safety pins or ball-point pens all over it.

6. *Buckskin Jacket and Quilted Skirt*

   Dollar bills pinned on jacket; a bedspread made into a skirt (quilt) or cotton balls pinned on skirt.

7. *Slip-on Sweater with Matched Pants*

   A sweater with a slip over it and pants with matchbooks all over.

8. *TV Jacket (for men)*

   A robe with *TV Guides*, antennas, etc. all over it.

9. *Smoking Jacket*

   Get a smoke bomb to release under the coat so there is smoke coming out the sleeves, etc.

FINE, AND YOU?

Here's a skit that is designed for use at Thanksgiving. It is based on the idea that it would be interesting to know what things would have been like if the Indians had gone to Europe and discovered the Pilgrims, instead of vice versa. This basic premise should be explained to the audience to set up the skit. The scene is somewhere in Europe. Five pilgrims are busy at work when an Indian walks in.

Indian:	How?
Pilgrim 1:	How what?
Indian:	How you doing?
Pilgrim 2:	Oh! Fine, and you?
Pilgrim 3:	Say, who are you? You don't look like you're from this area.
Indian:	I am chief of Sue Bee Indians. I am called Running Water.
Pilgrim 4:	Why "Running Water"? Do you have a Leaky Faucet?
Indian:	Yes, my cousin. He been here before?
Pilgrim 5:	No, you're the first Indian we've ever seen. Where are you from?

Pilgrim 1:	And how did you get here?
Indian:	How?
Pilgrim 2:	Fine, and you?
Indian:	I sail wide river called Atlantic in trusty canoe called April Shower.
Pilgrim 4:	There's another funny name. Why did you call your canoe "April Shower"?
Indian:	Silly Pilgrim. Don't you know that "April Shower bring Mayflower"?
Pilgrim 3:	You still haven't told us where you're from.
Pilgrim 5:	Well, he said he sailed across the Atlantic. But of course, we all know that he couldn't come from there since the world is flat and you'd fall if you went in that direction.
Pilgrim 3:	Well, maybe he crawled up the edge.
Pilgrim 1:	We must be more courteous to our guest. After all, we are preparing to celebrate our harvest.
Indian:	Really? How?
Pilgrim 2:	Fine, and you?
Pilgrim 1:	We set a large table full of food that we have harvested from our crops, such as corn (*holding up an ear of corn*).
Indian:	Ah, maize.
Pilgrim 4:	I just don't understand where you foreigners come up with such funny names for things. I mean, how can you do that?
Indian:	How?
Pilgrim 2:	Fine, and you?
Pilgrim 5:	Say, Leaky Faucet . . .
Pilgrim 4:	No, no, that's his cousin's name. He's Running Water.
Pilgrim 5:	Well, Leaky Faucet or Running Water. What's the difference? I mean, both names are All Wet.
Indian:	No. My uncle called All Wet.
Pilgrim 3:	You must have a lot of rain back home. I'll have to make you an umbrella to take back with you.
Indian:	Make umbrella? You know how?
Pilgrim 2:	Fine, and you?
Pilgrim 5:	Hey, listen, Running Water. I wanted to ask you, do you Indians plant other things besides corn—like potatoes, pumpkins, and squash?
Indian:	Oh, yes. But it take long time to plant all these things.
Pilgrim 3:	Well, goodness. We're able to plant things real fast.
Indian:	Oh? How?
Pilgrim 2:	Fine, and you?

Pilgrim 3:	We use a plow to break up the soil and make the planting faster.
Pilgrim 1:	We would be glad to share this knowledge of the plow with you and your family.
Pilgrim 4:	Oh, isn't it wonderful to be able to share things with new people from different places.
Indian:	And how!
Pilgrim 2:	Fine, and you?
Pilgrim 1:	Running Water, won't you join us as we celebrate our harvest festival?
Pilgrim 5:	Yes, we always have so much that God has given us: good food, good times, good friends.
Pilgrim 3:	I suppose we have so much to be thankful for.
Indian:	Yes, This is time of . . . Thanksgiving.
Pilgrim 4:	Thanksgiving! Now, there's one Indian name I really like. I think we should make this a national holiday. (*To Pilgrim 2*) Don't you think so?
Pilgrim 2:	Well, yes. But how?
Indian and other Pilgrims:	Fine, and you?

HOT DOG

This skit requires only one person, who is talking on the telephone. The audience, of course, hears only one side of the conversation. The props needed are a play telephone and a uniform from a fast-food restaurant.

Hello! This is Richard's Foods-to-Go.
Yes, we had an ad in the paper for dogs for sale.
Well, we have some a foot long and some smaller.
They came Wednesday. So they've been here about four days.
Oh, yes, they all came at the same time.
What? You thought the larger ones came first?
What color? They're all red.
Yes. We can have some ready for Christmas. You want what? One for Judy, one for Jimmy, and one for Joey. Whatever you say.
What was that about them being broken?
No, lady, the ones that are broken, we don't sell.
What do we do to keep the drippings off the floor? We wrap them in a napkin.
Right now they're back here in a box.
I guess there are about fifty in a box.
Yes, ma'am, it is kinda crowded.
Do we have paper under them? Yes, there is paper under each row.
No, ma'am, we don't take the papers out until we sell them. What did you say? I should be reported?
45¢ small and 75¢ foot-long.
Yes, we think that is a good price too.

Registered? No, ma'am, but they have been inspected.

Yes, we think that is just as good, too.

Look, lady, I'm talking about *hot* dogs.

You don't care about their temperature?

Hair? Lady, our dogs do not have hair on them. Yes, I said no hair.

No, they will not grow any later. I told you these . . .

You don't want any sick dogs? You think they are sick because of their high temperature?

Lady! These are hot dogs? *Hot dogs!* HOT DOGS!

Yeah, well, same to you! (*Hangs up*)

MEET MR. WOLF

Characters:	Luther Capehart, the host
	Mr. John A. Wolf, the wolf
Props:	Two chairs, a coffee table or a plastic plant.

Luther: Hello and welcome to "Put Up or Shut Up," a talk show where we try to interview all the newsmakers and the headline breakers. With us tonight is a truly startling manifestation of nature, a quirk of life, a chink in the armor of normality. Mr. John A. Wolf is with us and he claims that he is actually a wolf.

Wolf: That's right.

Luther: Let me get this straight. You claim that you are a four-footed, live-in-the-woods-type wolf, yet here you are two-footed, sitting erect, wearing a very nice suit . . . I don't understand. How is it possible?

Wolf: Well, when I was very young, just a pup, you might say, I was bitten by a gypsy.

Luther: I beg your pardon?

Wolf: Do you remember the movie *The Wolfman*? Lon Chaney was bitten by a wolf and he turned into a wolf. When I was just a pup, I was bitten on the ear by a gypsy. Now, every alternate Thursday, I turn into a human being.

Luther: I see . . . I think.

Wolf: I can still remember lying around the den, listening to my father spin his tales. Terrifying stories of wolves, like us, he'd insist, who'd been bitten by gypsies and transformed into human beings. Oh, how we laughed! There was a poem he taught us:

> Even a wolf who hunts in a pack
> And howls at the moon each night
> May become man every other Thursday
> If he's felt the wrath of a gypsy's bite.

If only I'd believed him!

Luther: There's probably a lesson here for all of us.

Wolf: I suppose.

Luther:	So, tell me, how did you happen upon this gypsy?
Wolf:	One day mom was taking us pups for a romp in the woods. I'm not clear as to how it happened, but before I knew it I was lost. A band of gypsies found me by the side of the road and took me in.
Luther:	A band of gypsies.
Wolf:	A marching band. They were on their way to the Rose Bowl Parade. The tuba player let me ride in the back of his van. I was playing with his three-year-old son when the kid bit me.
Luther:	And that bite caused you to become a man.
Wolf:	That was it.
Luther:	What happened after your first transformation?
Wolf:	Well, for one thing, I had a lot of trouble holding down a job.
Luther:	Because you could only be there every other Thursday?
Wolf:	Right. But I've worked that out.
Luther:	How?
Wolf:	I work with the police now.
Luther:	The police?
Wolf:	Yes, in the K-9 corps. Every other Thursday I'm my own partner.
Luther:	I see. Is that some sort of police identification around your neck?
Wolf:	Yes, this one is.
Luther:	What's that other? An official decoration for valor in the line of duty?
Wolf:	No. It's my flea-and-tick collar.
Luther:	Fascinating! I really want to thank you for coming by tonight. I hope our staff has made you comfortable in your stay.
Wolf:	They have, yes. But it really wasn't necessary to put all those newspapers on the floor of my dressing room.
Luther:	No problem at all. It really has been delightful having you here. (*Luther rises and walks to Wolf's side. He pets Wolf's head.*) You're such a nice puppy. (*Offering his hand*) Shake, boy. Come on, shake. (*They shake hands.*) (*To audience*) That's all for "Put Up or Shut Up" tonight. Thanks and we'll see you later. (*To Wolf*) Come on, boy, heel. Heel! (*They walk off stage.*)

PING PONG SKIT

Find two guys who can make loud "clicks" in the roofs of their mouths with their tongues, a sound like a ping-pong ball with a paddle.

They each hold a paddle and begin playing on an imaginary table, making the sound effects with their mouths. They gradually get farther and farther apart, making the "clicks" farther apart, too.

Finally, they get so far apart, they disappear offstage (or exit out side doors). When they reappear, they have switched positions and walk in backwards, continuing their game; but now it looks like they are hitting the ball all the way around the world. They continue playing and walking backwards toward each other until they bump into each other, turn around, and play a fast game facing each other as before.

THE ROLLER SKATER

Characters: Luther Capehart, affable talk show host
Josiah P. Forbes, roller skate man

Props: Two chairs; maybe a coffee table or a plastic plant; roller skates

Luther:	Hello and welcome to "Put Up or Shut Up," a talk show where we interview all the top-name performers and newsmakers. (*Remembering his guest he almost apologizes to the audience*) And, sometimes, when they're not available we talk to *you*, the ordinary citizen. My name is Luther Capehart and tonight we have with us a very ordinary citizen, Mr. Josiah P. Forbes. Mr. Forbes is, at this very moment, in the process of setting the world record for wearing a pair of roller skates.
Forbes:	(*eager*) I sure am!
Luther:	Welcome, Mr. Forbes.
Forbes:	Thank you. It's nice to be here.
Luther:	It's nice having you here.
Forbes:	Well, it's nice being here.
Luther:	(*trying to get down to business*) I think, Mr. Forbes, we should, at the very outset of the show, point out that you are wearing your roller skates not on your feet, as one might imagine, but on your hands.
Forbes:	That's right.
Luther:	Why is that?
Forbes:	Do you mean, why am I wearing these skates on my hands instead of on my feet?
Luther:	Exactly.
Forbes:	I don't know how to skate.
Luther:	But it says here that you are in the process of setting a world record for—
Forbes:	(*interrupting*)—for wearing roller skates. Doesn't say anything about feet, does it?
Luther:	No.
Forbes:	I wouldn't have lasted 87 minutes with these things on my feet.
Luther:	(*resigned*) And how long have you lasted?
Forbes:	87 days.
Luther:	87 days.
Forbes:	87 days.

Luther:	Certainly is a long time.
Forbes:	I want to set a record that will be hard to break. I plan to keep these skates on until Arbor Day.
Luther:	How long will that make it?
Forbes:	I'm not quite sure. Actually, I was hoping you could tell me.
Luther:	Tell you what?
Forbes:	When is Arbor Day?
Luther:	(*pauses to think*) I'm afraid I don't know. (*another pause*) Perhaps you could visit your local library.
Forbes:	I tried that.
Luther:	And?
Forbes:	They threw me out. Ever try thumbing through a Britannica with roller skates on your hands? I ripped it up good.
Luther:	I bet you've run into a lot of little problems like that.
Forbes:	I sure have. One thing I found rather difficult was eating mashed potatoes.
Luther:	Keep slipping off your wheels, do they?
Forbes:	They sure do. And another thing is playing pinochle. Do you know how hard it is to shuffle cards with these things on?
Luther:	(*holding up a hand, signaling Forbes to stop*) I can imagine. Ha, ha. (*The voices of the two now begin to overlap as each man continues his own conversation: Luther, trying to wrap up the show, Forbes complaining.*)
Forbes:	Or making a phone call? Do you know how hard that is? And try explaining to an operator why you're not dialing direct.
Luther:	That's just fine.
Forbes:	It's near impossible.
Luther:	Well, thank you for joining us tonight, Mr. Forbes. It certainly was a pleasure.
Forbes:	Or playing ping-pong?
Luther:	(*to audience*) That's all for now folks. Tune in again next time for more of "Put Up or Shut Up."
Forbes:	You can't hold a paddle with a roller skate on your hand.
Luther:	(*looking off stage*) Are we off? Good.
Forbes:	Just try putting some spin on a ping-pong ball while you're wearing a roller skate on your hand. (*Luther exits. Forbes follows still complaining.*)
Forbes:	It can't be done! It just can't be done!

THE SEAGULL AND THE SURFER

Here's a spontaneous skit that demands no props nor preparation. The "characters" can be chosen on the spot. Their instructions are simple. As the narrator reads the story slowly, each "character" is to act out what is being described. For example:

"The waves rise in great swells." (The people who are "waves" begin to rise up and down.) Be sure the narrator gives the "actors" enough time to do what is being described.

Characters: Sun
Seagulls (any number)
Waves (any number)
Surfer
Shore (any number)

It's a bright and beautiful morning at the beach. The *sun* is rising slowly, and the *seagulls* are waking up after a long night's rest; the *waves* are calm and serene, and the *shore* is smooth and damp.

The ocean world now seems to come alive as the *seagulls* chatter to each other and fly off on their morning search for food. As the *gulls* are flying over the *shore* and *waves,* they begin to get playful. They soar higher and higher, then drop suddenly skimming the *waves* with their outstretched wings. They fly up, then up, then up and down again, in circles, in zigzags, backwards, then forwards. The *gulls* are chattering noisily, screaming as loud as they can. Suddenly, the playfulness ends and the *gulls* return slowly to their nests to rest.

The *waves* are beginning to rise in great swells. They rise higher and higher reaching farther and farther until at the last second they come crashing down on each other and roll on to the *shore.*

A *surfer* arrives at the beach, stepping on the *shore.* Excited at the prospect of the big *waves* which are continuing to break on the *shore,* the *surfer* begins to jump up and down. He sits on the *shore* and gazes at the breaking *waves.*

The *surfer* now decides to take his board out into the water. He paddles out, making fast, long strokes. He paddles faster and faster with longer and harder strokes until he gets past the *waves.* He uses his skill to dodge in and out of the *waves* with precision timing. He is full of poise and grace as he "hangs ten" on his surfboard. Then suddenly a *wave* grabs him and sends him crashing into the *shore.*

The *surfer,* now tired and beaten, gathers up his surfboard and slowly stumbles away from the *shore* and heads for home.

Day is coming to an end as the *sun* sets slowly. The *birds* make their last flight, flying over the *shore* and *waves* and once again return to their nests for a cozy night's sleep, tucking their wings under their bodies and lowering their heads.

As we take one last look at the beautiful ocean scene before the *sun* sets, we can see the restful *seagulls* and the *waves* beating on the *shore.*

THE TOMB REVISITED

This is a modern version of the Easter story. It's not very appropriate for a solemn morning service, but it's great as a creative way to introduce a story people may be overly familiar with. It has good discussion possibilities.

Characters:	Guards: Louie, Bernie, Marvin, Norman Chief Priests: Caiaphas, Annas
Setting:	Four guards are sleeping in front of Jesus' tomb. They are to snore and awaken without paying any attention to the tomb.

SCENE I

Louie:	(*Wakes up, rubs eyes, yawns, and stretches*) Man is it cold out here—I'd better build a fire. (*Begins to rub two sticks, puts wood and leaves together, blows into it, etc.*)
Bernie:	Hey, watcha doing Louie?
Louie:	Oh, just putting my Boy Scout training to use.
Bernie:	Forgot the matches again, eh? (*Gets up and goes over to a knapsack and finds a box of matches.*) Here ya go. (*Throws matches to Louie.*)
Marvin:	(*Awakening from sleep*) Hey, what's going on with all the noise?
Louie:	(*Testily*) I'm trying to get a fire going for breakfast.
Marvin:	Never mind for me—I've got mine all ready to go. (*Shows a box of cereal and begins to prepare his own breakfast.*)
Norman:	(*Who has by this time also awakened—sniffs in the air as if something is burning.*) Hey, what's burning?
Louie:	Probably wood.
Norman:	(*Walking toward fire*) No, no. It smells like something rotten is burning. (*Pause*)
Bernie:	Oh, it's just your imagination.
Marvin:	No—I smell something now too.
Louie:	What's that in the fire there? (*Pokes a stick in the ''fire'' and pulls out a burned shoe.*)
Norman:	Those are my new Adidas you've been using for kindling wood, you idiot. Why, I ought to strangle you with my bare . . . (*This last line is said while chasing Louie around the fire. Louie falls at Norman's knees, wraps his arms around him, and begs for mercy.*)
Louie:	Please, Norman—have mercy on me.
Bernie *and Marvin:*	Yeah, Norman, give him a break. (*Just then Norman notices the empty tomb. His eyes bug out and he says:*)
Norman:	Look! The tomb! It's empty!
Everyone:	We're in big trouble.
Marvin:	We are all gonna get fired.
Louie:	(*Crying*) I'm going to lose my pension—and I only had three more years to go until retirement.
Bernie:	Don't feel bad. I've got a house to pay for and a son attending Jerusalem State Medical School.

Norman:	What are you guys talking about? It's not our fault that the tomb is empty. Jesus must have really come back from the dead—just as He predicted.
Louie:	What makes you say that, Norman?
Norman:	That rock moved! Who do you think moved it—the tooth fairy?
Marvin:	(*Glaring at Bernie*) We wouldn't have slept through an earthquake.
Bernie:	Well, don't look at me—I don't know where Jesus is.
Louie:	Well, if it's not our fault that He's gone, let's get down to headquarters and tell the chief priests to put out an APB.
Everyone:	Right! (*Pick up sleeping bags, put out fire, etc. as curtain closes.*)

SCENE II

The setting is a room with a desk and chairs, depicting the place of the chief priests.

Caiaphas:	(*Excitedly*) What are you guys doing here? You're supposed to be at the tomb!
Louie:	(*Nonchalantly*) There's nothing there to guard. Jesus is gone.
Annas:	(*Very excitedly*) Gone! Where did He go?
Marvin:	Norman thinks that Jesus has risen from the dead—just like He predicted He would.
Annas:	You nincompoops! We can't have people believing Jesus came back from the dead. Think what it will do to our religion and, more importantly, to all of our jobs! Why, who is going to give to the temple if they think there is a risen Savior?
Bernie:	Well, what do you want us to do?
Caiaphas:	Let us think about it for a minute. (*Caiaphas and Annas huddle for a few moments.*)
From the middle of the huddle:	That's a good idea.
Caiaphas:	(*Coming back to the guards*) Look, who else knows about Jesus' rising from the dead?
All the guards:	Nobody.
Caiaphas:	(*Rubbing his hands together*) All right, this is what we are going to say to the press. Quote: "We do not know the whereabouts of Jesus of Nazareth's body, because while the guards were sleeping, His disciples stole Him away."
Norman:	That's no good. If we were sleeping, how would we know His disciples stole the body?
Annas:	(*Testily*) Norman, we're doing this for you as well as for ourselves. This statement will not only save your job but will also make you rich.

Norman:	(*Sarcastically*) How?
Annas:	(*Pulls out a wad of money*) This money is for you—if you can keep our little secret. Do I have any takers, boys?
Bernie:	(*Greedily stuffs money in pockets*) I've got a boy in medical school.
Louie:	I need a little extra for my retirement. (*Stuffing money into his pockets*)
Marvin:	Everybody likes money.
Norman:	(*Firmly*) Money never brought a man back from the dead though. (*Exits right, leaving the other standing in the room with blank looks on their faces*)

TOM MEETS GOD

Here's a short skit with a message. It requires three actors and should be well rehearsed before presentation to the group. Follow up the skit with a discussion of what happened. Although this skit is quite short, there are several issues raised worth getting into.

Tom:	(*Knocks and an "angel" opens the door*) Hi! My name is Tom. I would like to see the person in charge please.
Angel:	Sure, come on in.
Tom:	Look, aah, I know this guy is really important, but do you think He would see someone like me?
Angel:	He sees everyone. You can see Him any time you'd like.
Tom:	Could I see Him now?
Angel:	Go right on in.
Tom:	Now?
Angel:	Yes.
Tom:	(*Hesitating and then slowly walks in*) Uh, excuse me, my name is Tom. I wondered if I could see You for a few minutes?
God:	My name is God and I've got all the time you need.
Tom:	Well, I'm going to high school right now, and I am a little confused about what I should do. . . . A couple of my friends say you can help, but they seem just as confused as I am. To be quite honest, I haven't really been impressed by Your work. I mean, don't get me wrong, my friends are really good friends, you know, and they really seem to like me, but they haven't got it so good. Bob, one of my friends, has a dad who is an alcoholic, and my other friend's folks are getting a divorce. The crazy thing is my folks are great, I really love them, and everything's going great . . . except . . . except I can't seem to see the point in life. In spite of all the junk that is happening to my friends, they seem to be convinced that You are important. So that's why I'm here. I just thought You could give me some pointers. I just feel kinda lost.
God:	My price is high.
Tom:	That's ok, because my folks are pretty well off. What is it?
God:	All.

Tom:	All?
God:	Yes, all. Everything.
Tom:	Sheesh. Don't you have a lay-away plan? How about a pay-as-you-go? Isn't Your profit margin a little out of line?
God:	Actually, My cost was quite high also . . . ask My Son.
Tom:	Well, uh, I think I'll have to wait awhile. I appreciate Your taking the time to talk to me and I'm sure You're worth it. It's just that at my age, it's a little too soon to give up everything. After all, when you're young that's when the good times happen. Besides, I think I can get what I'm looking for at a much cheaper price.
God:	Be careful, Tom. The price may be cheaper, but your cost may be much higher than you think.
Tom:	Yeah, sure. Well, nice talking to You, God. Maybe I'll see You around sometime.
God:	Yes, Tom, and there's no maybe about it.

TV CHRISTMAS STORY

Here's a dramatic presentation that can be given at Christmas time centered around a television newscast. The newscast occurs on the first Christmas day but is done with a modern set. Simply reproduce a large TV news set complete with monitor, station call letters in the background, etc. You could even go so far as to construct phony cameras, etc. All of the news commentators should be dressed in modern clothes. Feel free to adapt, add to, or subtract any part of the script.

Characters:

Announcer	Martha Waltersberg
Commercial Announcer	Mort Solomon
Barnabas Cronkite	Eric Rosen
Moshe Smith	Stud Barjonas
David Saul	

Announcer:	Stay tuned for the VBS Evening News with Barnabas Cronkite with the latest on a strange sighting in the sky; Martha Waltersberg from downtown Bethlehem, where a huge crowd is gathering for the tax enrollment; and Dr. Ben Hadad with reports about a new cold front moving in. That's the VBS news coming up next.
Commercial Announcer:	Taxes. Taxes. Taxes. No one likes to pay taxes. But H & R Blockberg is the only tax-consulting service authorized by the Roman government, *and* each and every consultant has previous tax-collecting experience. Yes, you can trust H & R Blockberg for all your tax-related problems. H & R Blockberg, 700 Appian Way.
Announcer:	The VBS Evening News with Barnabas Cronkite in Jerusalem, Martha Waltersberg in Bethlehem, and Dr. Ben Hadad on Mt. Ararat. Brought to you by Hertz Donkey Rental—the donkeys O. J. Feldman rides—and Gethsemane Nurseries, with gardens in every major city. Now . . . Barnabas Cronkite.

Barnabas:	Good evening. There has been a new development on the strange light that has been sighted in the Eastern hemisphere for the last few nights. Correspondent Moshe Smith reports.
Moshe:	For the past few nights a bright light or starlike phenomenon has been appearing in the sky. At first it was thought to be a meteor or an optical illusion, but tonight Dr. Ishmael Streisand confirmed that what everyone is seeing is, in fact, a star. The question is, Where did this star come from and what does it mean? Officials close to the situation are speculating that the star is not an isolated incident and that more strange occurrences may be expected. Concerned government officials are monitoring the situation closely, and reliable sources have told VBS that other similar incidents have not been made public. This is Correspondent Moshe Smith in Jerusalem.
Barnabas:	VBS News has learned that an incident did occur near Bethlehem, and we now switch to our mini-cam live in the hills of Bethlehem. David Saul reports.
David:	Barnabas, approximately ten minutes ago a group of shepherds told me that they saw some kind of an angel accompanied by music and bright lights. Normally stories from shepherds are discounted because of the fact that they are a strange breed . . . and tend to hit the sauce . . . *but* government officials here seem strangely concerned. From my discussions with the shepherds, apparently they think this has something to do with a Messiah promised years ago. The mention of the Messiah seems to have government officials concerned. From the hills of Bethlehem, this has been David Saul reporting.
Barnabas:	We'll be right back after this message from Hertz.
Commercial Announcer:	O. J. Feldman here for Hertz. When you're in a strange town, it's nice to know your friends at Hertz are ready to help. Maybe you had to trade in your donkey for tax money, or maybe yours kicks people in crowds. That's the time to rent a donkey from Hertz. Our donkeys are used to crowds and are guaranteed to get you where you want to go. Of course, Hertz uses nothing but fine GMAC donkeys. Hertz—where we treat donkeys like donkeys and treat you right.
Barnabas:	Last month Caesar Augustus issued a decree requiring all citizens to return to their city of birth in order to attain an accurate enrollment for taxing. Martha Waltersberg is in Bethlehem for the story.
Martha:	I'm standing here at the No Room Inn on the outskirts of Bethlehem. Thousands of people are swarming into the city now and every available facility is full. Just a few minutes ago a woman who is about to have a baby was almost turned away. Finally, after protests from her husband, they were allowed to stay with the animals. We just finished talking with the head of the Best Eastern Lodge Association, and he suggests that anyone heading for Bethlehem attempt to find lodging outside of town. The head of the Roman government here in Bethlehem is deeply concerned about crowd control. So far there have been no major incidents. The question is, Can this uneasy quiet continue? Martha Waltersberg at the No Room Inn in Bethlehem.

Barnabas:	A group of highly respected astrologers have begun a significant journey. Correspondent Mort Solomon reports from Peking.
Mort:	Walter, a large party of wealthy astrologers are traveling toward Israel to observe a strange light. Apparently it is the same strange light seen over Israel the past few weeks. Informed sources have told us that these men believe there is some relation between the light and the Messiah. Although there has been no official recognition by the Roman government, it is believed that when the astrologers arrive within Roman territory they will be summoned before government officials. Reporters here, Walter, are baffled as to this sudden concern on the part of Roman officials for this promised Messiah. Why, we just will have to wait and see. Mort Solomon from China.
Commercial Announcer:	The VBS News will continue in just a moment. Ladies, now is the time to order your hooded capes and robes. The Good Hood Company has an incredible selection now. These hooded capes and robes are all one piece of material so the hood cannot be lost nor can it become entangled in water jugs being carried on the head. The Good Hood Company—where we also have a clearance on beautiful sheepskin swimming suits. Come by and see us soon.
Barnabas:	Eric Rosen has been watching with interest the increasing speculation about a coming Messiah. Eric?
Eric:	The reason there is so much concern about a Messiah, of course, is the popular notion by the Jews that such a Messiah will become a political force and overthrow the Romans. This is a hope that Jews have had for years, and we have seen potential "Messiahs" come and go. We have a feeling that the strange light in the East is nothing more than a passing phenomenon that those who are overly religious and mystical can cling to or, worse yet, use to mount a revolutionary movement. I have done some research on this matter of a Messiah and I am not so sure that if and when such a Savior were to appear, He would be a political leader. I am sure I will get a lot of mail about this, but I think it would be much more profitable if those who are so anxiously awaiting a Messiah would start living as if they believed in the God they say they believe in. I guess it is always easier and less threatening to hope in the future than to live as if the future were now. Eric Rosen, VBS News.
Barnabas:	Jerusalem has been the home of the National Open Spear-throwing Olympics. Stud Barjonas reports.
Stud:	Coming off of major upset victories, two Hebrews will be facing each other in the finals to be held next Friday. Friday's match between Philip of Caesarea and Simeon of Bethany has already been sold out. There is some concern that Philip of Caesarea may have trouble keeping his feet within the specified boundaries on his approach. He refused comment on the two warnings he received today. However, sources close to Philip confirm that he will be wearing a new imported brand of sandal to give him additional footing. Should be quite a match. In chariot racing today, Fireball Jonah

narrowly escaped serious injury when his vehicle turned over in the north-west turn at the Hippodrome. This turn is considered one of the most hazardous in racing. In spite of the mishap, Jonah went on to win the main event.

Barnabas: Dr. Ben Hadad has been standing by on Mount Ararat for the weather report, but we have just received a bulletin from Bethlehem. Martha Waltersberg is there.

Martha: Walter, as you know from my earlier report, I am at the No Room Inn here in Bethlehem. Just as we were getting ready to leave, we were told of a commotion at the back of the inn. We found a young girl who had just given birth to a baby in the stable where they keep the animals. Normally, we would have ignored the story; but, Walter, something strange is occurring here. A huge crowd is gathering and a number of shepherds and others almost seem to be worshiping the baby. We have been unable to get any comment from anyone here, but there is one more thing. That strange light in the East seems to be much brighter now and almost seems to be directly above us. This is Martha Waltersberg in a stable in Bethlehem.

Barnabas: And that's the way it is. Barnabas Cronkite for the VBS Evening News. Good night.

Case Studies

Case Studies

The "case study" is a creative learning strategy which can be used effectively in Christian education. Properly done, case studies can involve youth or adults in a topic in ways that few other methods can.

Case studies have been used in colleges, graduate schools, and seminaries for years and are now filtering into the church where more and more church educators, youth directors, lay sponsors, and others are finding them helpful.

A case study is simply a description of a situation or problem faced by someone that requires analysis, decision, and planning. Case studies may be extremely long or relatively short. In the cases presented in this book each case involves several paragraphs. But it's not the length of the case that really matters. It's what the leader and the group do with it. Case studies are designed to teach students the art of decision-making under difficult conditions, and to fulfill this goal, the leader must know how to dissect a case study properly. The whole process involves helping the learners get inside the minds and hearts of the people mentioned in the case, to really feel and think what the people are thinking, to bring to the situation what they know as individuals, and to try and make mature decisions about the case.

In all the cases that follow, specific suggestions are given to help you and the group take apart the case. Here are some other suggestions:

1. *Make sure that everyone reads the case.* Give the group members enough time to finish.
2. *As a group, name aloud the principal people in the case (one at a time).* This is done aloud to make sure everyone knows who the characters are. If there is confusion at this point, the whole study will be unduly complicated.
3. *Have the group describe how they think each character in the case feels.* This is the first step toward getting into the hearts and minds of the principals in the case study.
4. *Role-play the situation.* Choose one of the key issues or confrontations in the case study and have some members of the group role-play what they would do. Role plays can be done in small groups of four to six or before the entire group.

Those not involved directly in the role play should observe what's going on. Two other rules in role playing are: (a) Don't limit people to sex roles. In other words, the males in your group don't always have to play male roles, nor females the role of women. (b) Cut off the role play when the essence of the dialogue has been reached, when you feel that the characters have exhausted their possibilities and have little more to contribute. Cut if off before the audience and the players tire of the play.

5. *Discuss after each role play.* This can be done in small groups or before the whole group. Structure some questions in advance.

Some basic questions that work with almost every role play are these:

1. Were the players realistic?
2. What helpful things did they say to one another?
3. What would you have said?
4. How did the role players feel?
5. What could the role players say and do differently?
6. If they could switch roles, what would they have said?

A case study that involves more than two characters can lend itself to many individual or group role plays as well. With these principles and the specific questions designed for the case studies in this book, you should find case studies effective for confronting issues and stimulating discussion.

A TIME TO LIVE, OR A TIME TO DIE

Did you ever have a nightmare that you couldn't wake up from? Or maybe it's more like being one of the main characters in a play and all of a sudden finding out that you never got a script. You're expected to have the answers to the big question, and the whole play stops, waiting for you to deliver the key lines. Except you don't have the answer; you don't know your lines.

Bill and I had been close friends since we were kids. My family moved into an apartment building when I was five; Bill lived underneath us. We were about the same age, and just naturally started hanging around together.

At first we were both kinda shy, my being new and all. But we wound up in the same room together in school, and because our last names began with the same letter, sat near each other. We walked to school and home again with the same gang, played the same games, stuff like that.

Somehow we never seemed to fight. I don't know why. We'd disagree on things but never let our differences come in the way of our friendship. By the time we got to high school we were pretty much accepted as a pair, or maybe a *team* is a better word. There was always a big gang of us in the neighborhood; we both had a lot of friends; but when it came to best friends, there was no doubt; it was Bill and I.

Bill got his driver's license the summer before his junior year. At first I was worried; I was six months younger than he was and thought he might start hanging around with other kids who could drive too, especially when his older sister "handed down" her car to him. It didn't work out that way, though. We still hung around together as much as before, if not more; we could go a lot more places with wheels. We even double-dated sometimes; though, since we both had jobs, Bill at a shoe store, me at a drive-in restaurant, we didn't do it much.

Why is it that things can go along so well and then the bottom falls out of everything? Neither Bill nor I had ever been really sick, broken any bones, or anything like that. We were both pretty healthy. And then Bill had his accident.

It was a Friday night. I was working, but Bill had the night off and had a date with a girl he had been going with for a couple of months. They had gone out to the drive-in theater and stayed late. Bill dropped her off at about midnight and then headed home. It was late and Bill had to be at work at 9:00 that morning: I guess he was in a hurry and going a little fast. That really doesn't matter any more.

Bill must have hit the tracks south of town sooner than he expected; they're in bad shape and can screw you up if you're not careful. I guess Bill wasn't. He shot over the tracks and lost control of the car. There's a concrete wall this side of the drainage ditch that borders the road. Bill hit it head-on.

They found him at about 4:00 A.M.. It was a back road and nobody was out at that time in the morning. Bill's folks had gone to bed earlier; they trusted him to set his own curfew. He must have lay in that ditch for at least a couple of hours. Thank God he couldn't feel anything. Maybe that's the best way to describe what happened—he couldn't feel anything. The doctors said later that he had "severed his spinal cord"; that's a fancy way of saying he broke his neck. Bill was alive, from the neck *up*.

Bill's mother called me at 7:00 that morning from the hospital. She was crying. She had been with Bill since 4:30; Bill's father was still with him in the intensive care ward. She told me what happened and what was wrong with Bill. My parents drove me down to the hospital immediately, but Bill was unconscious. They tried to comfort Bill's parents, who were really in bad shape; there wasn't much that I could do but sit and think.

I didn't know what was wrong with Bill, but figured he was dying. I don't know if you've ever had someone close to you dying, but it's strange the thoughts that go through your mind. They're mostly selfish thoughts: What will I do without Bill? I miss him already. Stuff like that. You feel guilty too, guilty for thinking like that, guilty for not being able to do anything. I cried some.

Bill didn't die. The doctors said he should have, considering what happened. They had to put him in an iron lung to keep him breathing; meanwhile they called in all kinds of specialists and ran all kinds of tests to see how they could put him back together again. I visited him every day after school; his mother stayed with him day and night.

It was Friday again, three weeks after the accident. I was going up to the hospital; Bill and I were planning to watch a movie on TV together. I felt like I usually did when I approached Bill's room—under a lot of pressure, uncomfortable, even though Bill was my best friend. I just couldn't let Bill know how sad I was. I had to put up a front to keep him cheerful.

Before I got to the door, Dr. Carson, Bill's physician, came around the corner. He called to me to wait.

"Glad I caught you," he began. We had been friends for a while; both our families went to him. "I need to talk to you for a minute." We settled into two nearby chairs. He leaned forward and spoke softly.

"I guess the only way to do this is just say it. Bill is never going to get better. We can keep him alive for five, ten, maybe twenty years. Who knows. But he'll always be paralyzed, always have to use an iron lung."

You can't say much when you're hit with something like that. I mumbled something like "Won't they ever be able to do anything?" My eyes were getting kinda full.

"Miracles still happen, I suppose. Medical breakthroughs are still made. But right now we don't even have the slightest idea how to repair a severed spinal cord. It's completely beyond our capabilities," Dr. Carson replied.

I guess I must have looked pretty bad. Dr. Carson put his hand on my shoulder. "Bill has known this for two weeks. So have his parents. I didn't tell you because I wanted you to keep cheering Bill up. But you've got to know now. Bill asked me to tell you."

"How did Bill take it?" I couldn't think of anything else to say.

"Good, I think. We stressed that he could still finish high school, maybe even go home some day."

"But never without an iron lung?"

"No, he'll always have it with him. But Bill can still lead a useful life!" Dr. Carson leaned closer. "You'll have to give Bill the will to stay alive as long as he can. You're his best friend."

I felt like someone had just handed me a thousand-pound weight. How could I cheer up Bill? I was crying myself.

It took me another five minutes after Dr. Carson had left to pull myself back together. I guess I didn't do that good of a job; when I finally walked into Bill's room he knew right away what was wrong.

"Carson finally told you, didn't he?"

"Yeah. Why didn't *you* tell me sooner?"

"I couldn't. I knew how much it would hurt you, and I just couldn't face it."

I sat down in the chair next to Bill. "What next?" I grinned weakly.

Bill looked at me for what seemed like hours before he replied. "I guess if I can't tell you, then I can't tell anyone," he said finally. "I've had two weeks now to think about this. At first I just cried. Then I was angry. Angry at everyone. I got awfully depressed. But I've settled down now."

I was surprised and a little ashamed. "Bill, I never noticed any of that. You always seemed so cheerful and everything."

"I'm a good actor," he said wryly. "Look, I don't buy that stuff Carson dishes out about a useful life and all that."

"Yeah, he hit me with that too," I admitted.

"Let's face it," Bill continued. "I'll be paralyzed for the rest of my life. I can never leave this lung. The chances of my ever getting well are nonexistent. I will spend the rest of my life just like this, probably getting a little worse each year, until I die of pneumonia or something. Carson admitted that."

There wasn't much I could say. Bill continued, "This is my life. I am responsible for it. It's my decision whether I want to stay alive . . ."

"Bill," I interrupted, "what are you getting at?" I was afraid I knew what was coming.

"I've had a lot of time to think about this: I've looked at every possible angle. I've decided that I don't want to live anymore."

"But—." I started to object. My voice cracked, my eyes began to fill with tears again.

"Wait! This is my decision. I'm calm. I'm not all upset. I've thought about this for two weeks. It's *my* life. It's *my* decision."

I was scared, grasping for something to say. "What about your parents?"

"I tried to talk to them, but the minute I even mentioned that I wasn't sure that I wanted to stay alive, mom started crying and dad just got angry. Look, they're paying a thousand dollars a day to keep this machine going; our insurance only covers half of that. They love me, but they can't do that forever."

"I don't know what to say." I sure didn't.

"Let me put it this way. This has to be *my* decision. I'm the *only* one who has the right to make it. See this button?" Bill indicated a set of three buttons directly above his face on the front of the iron lung. One was marked "call," another "emergency," and the third "on-off." Bill was glancing at the on-off switch. "When you leave I'm going to turn this thing off. I can do it with my chin. I'll die quietly and quickly; it won't hurt; I can't feel much anyway. I want you to know. You've always been my best friend. I guess you could say that I love you. That sounds queer, but it doesn't matter how it sounds now." Bill turned his eyes so that he could look me square in the eyes. "I've considered all the options. My mind is made up. It's my decision."

I sat there staring at Bill, trying not to cry. All I could think of was the awful pain I felt. "Oh, it hurts!"

Focus Questions:

1. What should the youth telling the story do?
2. What are your reasons for saying that?
3. Do you have the right to kill yourself? Do others have the right to make you stay alive if you don't want to?

BLACK/WHITE

You are a white policeman in Selma, Alabama, in 1963. Your "beat" is the downtown section of the town.

As you are walking down the main street of Selma, you become aware of a disturbance outside of a drugstore. You quicken your pace to investigate the problem.

You push your way through the crowd to discover that there seems to be some sort of fight going on inside of the store. Going in, you find three middle-aged black women sitting at the lunch counter. The owner is standing before them brandishing an axe handle. He has refused to serve them and is demanding that they leave immediately. Seeing you, he orders you to enforce the law.

Selma city ordinance 38lb reads: "Individuals of non-Caucasian or mixed ancestry are to use *only* those facilities designated specifically for their use. It is the right of any proprietor of a licensed business establishment to determine what facilities, if any, are open to use by non-Caucasians."

Over the counter, a sign is posted reading "No Coloreds Served." There is a small bar-and-grill next to the drugstore which serves "coloreds."

As a Christian, you believe that all men are equal in the eyes of God. You have attempted to live this philosophy, treating blacks and whites alike. You have made both black and white friends over the years. You have opposed segregation whenever possible, though it hasn't been easy and though little progress has been made over the years.

The owner insists that you enforce the law. Doing so is enforcing segregation. As a Christian, you oppose segregation.

Learning to Listen:

Pair off and separate yourselves sufficiently from other groups so you can talk freely. Try to talk through the following questions using the following technique:

1. Let Person 1 respond to the question.
2. Person 2 should then tell Person 1 what he/she thinks that person was trying to say: "I heard you say that you feel. . . ."
3. Then, Person 1 should let Person 2 know how close he/she has come: "What I was trying to say was. . . ."

4. Person 2 should again respond: "I heard you say that you feel. . . ."
5. Person 1 again. Let Person 2 know if he/she is closer this time.

Do this as long as you need to, to satisfy Person 1 that Person 2 understands what he/she was trying to say. Then repeat the whole thing, letting Person 2 respond to the same question. Remember: *Never interrupt the other person.*

Focus Questions:

1. Put yourself in the policman's shoes. What feelings (not opinions or ideas, but emotions) are you experiencing?
2. List the options open to you (get as many as possible).
3. List the consequences of each of these options that you have listed. (What will happen if you try them?)
4. You have to make an instant choice. Choose one of your options. What reasons do you have for making that choice?
5. There was some kind of rule or guide that you used to make the choice. That is the basis for your "ethics." You may not be aware of it, but it exists. Try to put it into words.

SHADES

PART I:

Bill, Ann, and Sam are good friends. They are spending the weekend, along with other friends, at a retreat sponsored by the church. Sam has brought along his tape player and quite a few tapes, which he leaves out for everyone to use.

Bill and Sam had gone for a walk. As they were returning to the lodge, Sam stopped for a moment to talk to one of the sponsors. Bill went ahead, entering the lodge on his own. The building was empty except for Ann. As Bill walked in the room, he saw her quickly stuffing some of Bill's tapes into her suitcase.

Ann looked up, startled, at the sound of the screen door slamming behind Bill. She looked at him for what seemed like ages though it was only a few seconds. Both of them knew full well that she has been stealing Sam's tapes.

Before Bill or Ann could say anything to each other, they heard Sam's voice calling Bill's name. He was approaching the lodge. There was no way that Bill and Ann would have time to talk before Sam entered, nor was there time for Ann to put the tapes back, though she would have time to shut the suitcase with the tapes in it and hide it if Bill would let her.

Issues:

1. What are the options open to Bill in this situation?
2. What are the options open to Ann in this situation?

PART II:

Frank stopped by the local sporting goods store on his way to work to pick up some ping-pong balls to take to his youth group meeting later that night. As he rounded the corner of shelves, he saw another youth, whom he did not know, attempting to stuff a couple of handballs into his pocket. The other youth was startled by Frank's sudden appearance, but still managed to quickly pocket the handballs while he stared at Frank.

A split second after the youth had hidden the two handballs, a clerk, who had not seen any of what had happened, rounded the corner behind Frank and asked Frank if he needed any help.

Issues:

1. What are the options open to Frank in this situation?
2. What are the options open to the youth caught stealing?

PART III:

Abraham Cohen is a Jewish doctor living in Nazi Germany prior to World War II. Because of the Nazi's anti-Jewish laws, he is no longer allowed to practice medicine or to possess drugs or medicines of any kind.

Cohen's wife is dying of cancer. She is in terrible pain and has run out of narcotics to kill the pain. The German doctors in the area will not treat her because she is a Jew, nor will they give Cohen the drugs he needs to lessen her suffering.

Late one evening, Cohen left his wife in the care of his daughter and quietly went to the back of the local drugstore, where he picked the lock and stole inside. There, he began to collect the drugs he would need to treat his wife.

John Gotlieb, a policeman, had recently been hired by the owner of the drugstore as night watchman. As he made his rounds, he saw Cohen collecting the drugs. Though Gotlieb did not know Cohen personally, he knew who he was and all about the situation of his wife. Gotlieb had nothing against Jews and felt sorry for Cohen, but realized that if drugs were found missing that he, Gotlieb, would be questioned. As Gotlieb struggled with his indecision about what to do, Cohen, not knowing that Gotlieb had seen him, began to make his way toward the back door to leave.

Issues:

1. What other options (besides stealing) were open to Cohen?
2. What options are open to Gotlieb?
3. If Cohen finds out that he has been discovered by Gotlieb, what options are available to him?

Four Questions:

1. Go back, and in all three situations, quickly choose the option you would select if forced to make a decision.

2. Do you think a majority of people in our society would choose the same option as you did?
3. All three situations involved stealing. If your choice of options in all situations was the same, what does this say about the way you make decisions?
4. If you chose different options in different situations, what does this say about the way you make decisions?

Special Events

Special Events

BABY NIGHT

Have everyone bring a picture of himself or herself when he or she was one year old or younger. The name of the person should be on the back of the picture, and the picture should not have anyone else in it such as parents, brothers, sisters, or other relatives. Place the pictures on a bulletin board and number each picture. Everyone is to number a piece of paper according to the numbers on the board and decide who each baby is. You can also vote on:

1. Most beautiful baby.
2. Most likely to cry.
3. Most likely to break new toys in one day.
4. Most likely to get out of training pants first.

BLIND CAR RALLY

This is a great activity that combines both youth and adults in a fun learning experience. Divide into groups of threes and fours, and assign each group to a separate car. Blindfold each of the kids, put them in their assigned cars and then give the driver (an adult) a map of the route he is to take. Each driver should be given a different location from the others, but each location should be approximately the same time and distance from the starting point.

As each car travels its preassigned route, the driver is not allowed to converse with anyone in the car in any way. The blindfolded kids in the car can converse and guess all they want as to where they are going. Once a car reaches its destination, the passengers are taken out of their cars, walked around it twice, then driven back to the starting point. Everyone then removes their blindfolds and each group tries to identify on a map the exact route traveled. The group that determines the most number of streets actually traveled wins a prize.

BROAD SIDE OF A BARN

On a warm summer night show a movie on the side of a building, barn, or storage building. You can do this at camp also. It works great and the kids really like it.

CANDLELIGHT DINNER AT McDONALD'S

Here's an idea your youth group will not soon forget. The local press will enjoy it as well. Check with the management of your local McDonald's and reserve a special section of the restaurant at a specified time. Send out formal invitations to the group. Set the tables with white tablecloths, candles, and flowers. Prepare fancy menus and encourage the young people to dress formally. You may even want to provide a musical serenade and waiters.

THE CYCLOTRON

Here's how you can make a chilling, breath-taking thrill ride like that of an amusement park for your youth group. For a little time and money you can create a safe "Cyclotron" that they will want to ride again and again.

Materials: You need a large wooden spool, available from your phone company or water-and-power department. Some power companies sell used spools quite inexpensively. The best dimensions are those shown. Make sure it's sturdy. You also need sections of 2-inch galvanized pipe cut to size and threaded, two 2-inch side-outlet elbows, and four 2-inch caps.

You will also need two 3/4-inch pipe lengths (for hand grips), four 3/4-inch flanges, plenty of 16d common nails, two heavy duty seat belts, a lot of foam rubber, and various bolts and handles.

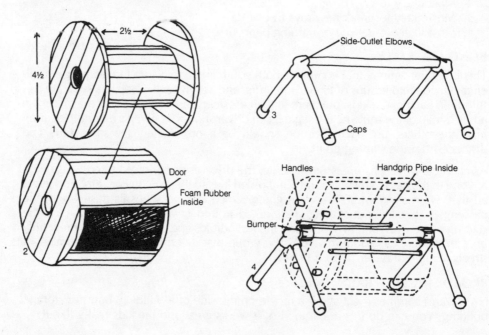

Now follow these simple instructions:

1. Take out the horizontal boards of the inner part of the spool.
2. Nail these same boards around the outer edges of the wheels, forming a large cylinder. Nail each board securely with three or four nails at each end. You will probably need more boards the same size from another spool. Nail them close together, leaving an opening about 2 feet wide for getting into and out of the cyclotron.
3. Pad the entire interior with thick foam rubber.
4. The pipe framework will look as shown, but don't assemble it yet. Put the horizontal pipe through the Cyclotron first, through the holes in the large wheels, then attach the other pipe fittings. The legs should be long enough to lift the cyclotron a few inches off the floor (it depends on the size of the spool you start with). The Cyclotron should now roll vertically on the sturdy pipe framework.
5. Bolt the seat belts into the interior so that when people are sitting inside (with their heads completely in), the belts will fasten firmly across their waist.
6. Bolt the hand-grip pipes and flanges in a position where the riders can hang on tightly, a few inches from the center pipe and directly in front of them when they're sitting inside.
7. Fasten some handles securely to the outside of the large wheels so that it can be turned.
8. Cut some 4-inch pieces from a thick cardboard tube (about 3 inches in diameter) and mount them on the horizontal pipe near the side-outlet elbows, as bumpers.
9. Test everything carefully before anyone uses it to make sure it is *safe.* Seat belts especially should be firmly bolted, and all pipe fittings should be tight.

How It Works:

The Cyclotron can hold two adults or four children. If two ride, one steps in first and fastens his seat belt securely. Then the other person goes around to the other side. Roll the entrance opening toward him and let him step in while you hold it still. Make sure both fasten their seat belts tightly and hold on to the hand grip with both hands. They are sitting facing each other; one can spread his feet apart and the other can have feet together.

Keep everyone out of the way and use only dependable operators who care about safety. Grab the handles or wherever you can get a good hold, and begin spinning the Cyclotron around. The riders travel around and around inside, going upside down. After it goes a short while, let it slow down, then change direction and spin it the other way, so that each rider gets to go both head-first and feet-first.

Operating Tips:

1. Put a little motor oil on the horizontal pipe where the Cyclotron rests on it; it will spin easier. Oil it every few rides.
2. The main danger is someone falling out the opening by not being fastened in securely. Double-check the seat belts before operating every time. Enforce the rule that *riders are not to unfasten the seat belts until given permission to do so.* Be sure their heads are well inside.
3. You can hold the riders in an upside-down position for a little while.
4. Choose an agreed-on word or signal that the riders can give for emergency stopping.
5. If possible, build your Cyclotron in a place where it can be locked up when not in use, to prevent someone from using it without a leader present.

The Cyclotron can be an "asked-for" attraction at your youth meetings. Their enjoyment of it will last longer if you don't overuse it—maybe open it once a month, or make them earn tickets for rides. Paint it in bright colors and make it as fun as you can. Don't force anyone to ride, but most teens, even if hesitant, will try it if their friends urge them to.

FAST-FOODS PROGRESSIVE DINNER

This is a fun variation of an old favorite activity. Find a street with several fast-food restaurants and plan a progressive meal accordingly. Start with a salad at one restaurant (salad bar preferably), then move on to "hors d'oeuvres" (french fries, soup, chili, taco chips, etc.), then the main courses (tacos, pizza, fish, hamburgers, etc.). Let the kids decide on the route. (Note: You can allow them to divide up for the main course depending on their preference.) The more creative ideas you can come up with to visit as many places as possible, the better.

FUNGI HUNT

Here's another scavenger hunt activity, but this one has some new ingredients that make it especially fun for either junior- or senior-high groups. Divide up into carloads, give each group a list of items like the ones below, set a time limit, and offer a prize to the group completing the most items. The driver or any adult can be the "judge" to make sure the group doesn't cheat. Items can be taken in any order.

1. Go to a certain donut shop and buy a donut of your choice. Each donut must be brought back to the church with a bite taken out of it by the person who sold the donut to you.

2. Get thirty marshmallows of various sizes from a single block of homes. They must be brought back to the church. Limit: five marshmallows per house.

3. Get the whole group to sit in a tree for one full minute.

4. Go to the house of someone who is in your car. File quietly into the house and sit down at the kitchen table. In unison ask, "What's for dinner, mom?" As soon as the mother comes out of shock, you may file out.

5. Go to an ice cream place. Have one person order a milkshake asking if it could please be made without ice cream.

6. At a fairly long red signal, everyone get out of the car and run around it once and then get back in before the light turns green.

7. Buy a mushy greeting card.

8. Go to a grocery store and have each member of the group go up to the same checker and ask her where you would find a box of prunes. Space yourselves so she doesn't know you are all together. Be sure to thank her each time she tells you.

9. Go to a department store. Go up to a sales clerk and ask her where something is that is right across the aisle from her. Be serious when you ask.

10. Go to the house of one of the individuals in your car. Everyone file into the bathroom, shut the door, flush the toilet, and then everyone file out.

11. Go to a designated corner in town. Everyone get down on your hands and knees and pretend that you are all looking for someone's lost contact lens. Keep this up for about three minutes.

12. Go to a restaurant and have everyone gather around the waitress of your choice and sing, "For she's a jolly good waitress".

13. Go to a designated house and have each person march in and shake hands with the man of the house. As you shake his hand, each person must say, "Sure is good to see you, sir."

14. Can you stuff everyone from your car into a phone booth? Try.

15. Go to a certain mall and ask a tall bald man what time it is.

16. Go to a gas station and seriously ask directions to the place right across the street from that particular gas station.

17. Get a pair of swim fins, then walk through a store holding hands with the person in the middle of your group wearing the swim fins.

18. Stand in front of the city hall and sing, "My Country 'Tis of Thee" with your hand over your heart.

19. Buy an orange and get the checker at the market to autograph it for you.

GENERATION BUDDIES

Here is a super way to get your church's senior citizens and youth group better acquainted. Invite the youth and adults (sixty-five or over) to sign a card if they are interested in having a "Generation Buddy." After the cards are turned in, match one young person with one senior citizen or couple. Try to pair up people who don't know each other. Send each of the people involved a card with the name, address, telephone number, and birthday of his/her buddy. Encourage the youth to make the first move toward friendship and arrange a meeting at the church or somewhere else where they can get acquainted.

Every two or three months sponsor a "Generation Buddies Social" for all those involved in the program. The youth should provide transporation for their buddies. Try to plan activities that both groups would enjoy. This can be the means of establishing some very special friendships among those involved and can have positive repercussions throughout the rest of the church.

HALLOWEEN GIVE-AWAY

This idea not only benefits the community and the church, but will leave quite an impression on your young people.

This Halloween have each young person bring a costume and a pound of Halloween candy. Have a number of empty paper bags prepared. After the kids arrive in costume, instruct them to open their candy and divide it equally among the empty bags. Then add to the bags several good pieces of literature, which could include things like an introductory brochure about the church, a letter from the youth themselves (see example), and a modern translation New Testament.

HAPPY HALLOWEEN!

The "scary-looking" bunch that just rang your doorbell, shouting "trick-or-treat" are members of the local _____ church's youth group.

We wanted to take this rather unique opportunity to celebrate Halloween with your family in ways other than soaping your windows, or asking you for candy. We wanted to be able to share with you this Halloween. So we put together these little "goodie bags"—candy for the children and some interesting little booklets for everyone. It is our hope that this little "goodie bag" will be enjoyed by everyone in your family.

We hope that as you eat the candy, you will take time to look through some of the booklets. They contain some "good things," too.

Have a happy Halloween. We have enjoyed this opportunity to talk with you and want you to know that our church is especially interested in your family. If you don't already attend a church regularly, we would love to have you attend our services. If there is ever any way we can be of assistance to you and your loved ones, please feel free to call us.

132

We would suggest that you might find it effective if you not only let the kids know what you are planning but encourage them to give their own money to buy the candy and the books. It would probably mean more to them.

HALLOWEEN WAX MUSEUM

This is a great idea if you live in a city with a wax museum. If you check with the owner, you can probably talk him into letting your youth group into the wax museum after hours. Be sure you have adequate leadership to prevent any possible damage to the museum. Prior to your visit to the wax museum, show the kids one of the many wax museum horror films (available from Swank Motion Pictures, 201 S. Jefferson, St. Louis, MO 63122), then go to the museum.

INDOOR HAYRIDE

Here's a great idea for a way to have a hayride during bad weather or for a different way to go Christmas caroling. This way even groups in urban or suburban areas can experience a hayride.

Secure a school bus without seats, a panel truck, or a van and dump two feet of loose straw inside. Add an old-fashioned pump organ, banjo, or accordian for effect, and bring a supply of cider and fresh apples for refreshments. (CAUTION: Make sure there are windows for ventilation. The dust gets very dense without it!) When you are done, back up to a trash dumpster and sweep it all away.

MINI-MASTERS TOURNAMENT

Hold a golf tournament just like the pros, only do it on a miniature golf course. Have each person play three rounds, with the totals posted on a big blackboard after each round. Give trophies to the winners in both the boys' and girls' divisions for first, second, and third places. You might try to secure a miniature golf course for a flat fee, so that the kids can play cheaper.

POLAROID NURSERY RHYMES

Divide the group into teams and make sure each team has a Polaroid (instant) camera and plenty of film. Give the teams a list of twenty nursery rhymes with one word missing from each. Each team chooses eight nursery rhymes. Each nursery rhyme is given a number representing difficulty which will be used later to determine the winner. Each team is given a certain amount of time to go out and take pictures that best represent the missing word of the rhyme.

When everyone returns at the predetermined time, a panel of impartial judges select the winning pictures based on (1) correct answer, (2) originality, and (3) quality of picture. Each picture could receive as much as five points in each category or as little as one point. The total is then averaged by three and multiplied by the number representing the difficulty factor. The team with the highest number of points wins.

PORT SCAVENGER HUNT

If you have a major airport in your area, you might find this a lot of fun. You may also find out, however, that the airport officials won't consider your game quite so much fun; neither will many of the passengers at the airport. So be sure to brief your kids ahead of time *not* to be obnoxious, *not* to bother those who don't want to be bothered, and *not* to run. After you have done all that, then divide into teams, give them a time limit, and have everyone meet back at a predetermined location at the end of the time limit.

Give them the list below (You can probably think of other list possibilities as well) and start them all at the same time. It might be wise to separate the teams into different terminals so that the same people are not being bothered.

1. Find a businessman with a computer company. (Have him sign name and position.)
2. Have a stewardess sign her name.
3. Ask a Krishna person what the greatest value in life is. Write down his/her response.
4. Find an airline pilot who is going to Hawaii today—name and airline.
5. Find either a couple going on a honeymoon trip or a couple going on a business trip.
6. Find a policeman who is either bald or named Harry.
7. Find out what a first-class round-trip ticket to Hawaii costs.
8. Find someone with a pilot's license (other than an airline pilot).
9. Find someone who's going back to school on a plane. (Get name of person and school.)
10. Ask the lady at the information booth the question she gets asked the most.
11. How many tires does a 747 have?
12. What does VRF stand for and what is it used for?
13. Find a marine on leave from boot camp and ask him in one sentence to describe his "D.I."
14. Find a sailor who's never been on the ocean.
15. Find a maintenance man.
16. Get a shoe shine (be sure to pay him) and have the man sign here.
17. Find someone who is in a hurry and offer to help them carry their bags to the gate.
18. Count all the cabs in front of the terminal, then get one cabbie to sign.
19. Ask a Hertz employee to give you a rental agreement envelope with O.J. Simpson's name on it.
20. How much does a hot dog cost at the snack shop?

SAKAYAMANASHIMIYACOPASHIROGEEITIS

The above name of this game is simply a synthesis of family names from a specific church. You can use this name or you can have fun making up a name synthesized from families in your own church and then being able to pronounce the name.

This game is basically a complex relay race relying heavily on teamwork. At any point during the race a team can easily come from behind. We have reprinted below a sheet that each person would receive explaining the game. The map, of course, would be different for your church.

"Sakayamanashimiyacopashiromotogeeitis": a highly contagious disease mainly characterized by rapid deterioration of brain tissues. Symptoms include the severe paralysis of the arms and legs, rapid loss of weight and strength, and terminal idiocy.

There are two methods of treatment available. The traditional method of treatment is the quick and immediate removal of the head by decapitation. The other known treatment of this horrendous disease is the administration of a special antidote. This antidote is a hot dog and mustard, taken orally with liquid. WARNING: IF THIS ANTIDOTE IS NOT GIVEN TO THE PATIENT QUICKLY ENOUGH, THE TRADITIONAL METHOD OF TREATMENT MUST BE ADMINISTERED!

Personnel:

3 airplanes (one must be female)
1 helicopter (blindfolded)
1 patient (must be female)
1 radar
1 nurse

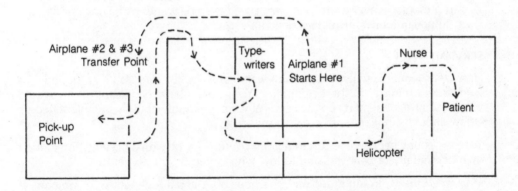

One member of your team has contracted the hideous disease, Sakayamanashimiyacopashiromotogeeitis. With all of your determination and strength of will, your main objective is to get the special antidote to your dying team member. The antidote must be flown in by plane, transferred to a helicopter, and taken to the hospital where the patient lies. The sequence is as follows:

1. Airplane No. 1 takes off from the starting point and gives the prescription to Airplane No. 2 at the transfer point.
2. Airplane No. 2 flies to pick-up point, receives the antidote, and returns to the transfer point. The pilot must exchange the prescription for the antidote.

3. The antidote is transferred to Airplane No. 3 (female) and flown back to the church accompanied by Airplane No. 1.
4. Before entering the airport (social hall), Airplane No. 2 must type the name "SAKAYAMANASHIMIYACOPASHIROMOTOGEEITIS". Typewriters are located in Burnett Hall. The airplane must enter the church through the stairs.
5. The antidote is given to the helicopter and brought to the hospital. Note: The helicopter encounters bad weather and must fly to the hospital blind. The pilot is guided in by radar.
6. At the hospital, the antidote is given to the nurse. Before this can transpire, the pilot must sign special authorization papers and give his name, address, phone and social security number to the nurse. The nurse must write the information on the chalkboard for identification purposes.
7. The nurse takes the antidote to the patient and assists her in taking the antidote. The first team to have their patient eat the hot dog and finish the drink will save their patient and be declared the winner.

Here are a few hints to help the game go smoothly:

1. Airplanes fly by running. The race is started when the "radar person" pops a balloon.
2. The "antidote" can be any food: hot dog, hamburger, taco, etc.
3. The patient's hands and legs are tied together to represent paralysis.
4. When the helicopter takes the antidote in, there could be a maze of chairs to represent a heavy storm. The game could even be wilder by having blindfolded "thunderclouds" disrupting helicopters.

SERVANT WEEK

Here is a summer activity that not only can involve all of your youth group, but is a witness and ministry to the community. Your particular schedule of events would vary, or course, depending on the needs of your community, but the sample schedule below should stimulate your creative thinking:

Sunday: Young people take part in regular church service with a presentation to their own community of believers and follow with coffee or refreshments.

Monday Morning: Youth group provides free coffee and doughnuts for commuters at train or subway location. If there are any left over, distribute them to local police stations, fire stations, city offices, or businesses.

Monday 10:00 A.M. – 4:00 P.M.: Entire youth group offers services to the city to provide help in an area that group determines is the greatest need. (The group that submitted this idea helped the city cut a trail in the city's open space—very difficult and back-breaking work.)

Tuesday: "Senior Citizens' Day". Have your youth group visit local nursing homes and provide programs such as talent shows, puppet shows, etc. Have the kids talk and play games with the elderly in these homes.

Tuesday Night: Sponsor a "Gay Nineties Sweet Shoppe" ice-cream party for the elderly of the church and the community.

Wednesday: "Children's Day". Plan activities for kids, such as puppet shows in the city park and at children's wards in hospitals. Offer free babysitting for couples to go out by themselves.

Thursday: "City Government Day". Kids can spend more time providing help and services to the city. End the day with an Appreciation Banquet put on entirely by the kids for the city leaders and business-people.

The above ideas are only suggestions, or course. Your group should find things to do every day that meet needs, demonstrate Christian love and concern, and are realistic (within the ability of the group to accomplish). The group that contributed this idea had a number of flyers printed which said in essence: "Hi, we're the youth group from (name of church) and we want to serve you if you will let us. We don't want to sell you anything, solicit a donation, or try to get new church members. We are just trying to learn to obey the Lord by serving. 'Through love, serve one another' (Galatians 5:13)."

If you spend time preparing well for "Servant Week," you'll find that not only will your youth group learn a lot, but they will grow closer to one another, and the community will benefit from many acts of kindness.

SERVICE ROCK-A-THON

A new dimension is added to the Rock-a-thon idea when the youth pledge an hour of service for every hour they rock. For example if twenty youth rock for 12 hours, the entire group pledges 240 hours of service. The group can then work off the time by visiting shut-ins, going on service retreats and work camps, doing yard work for the disabled, etc. Of course, you still get adult sponsors to give a certain amount of money per hour rocked, but the adults are much more willing to pledge if they know the youth are going to work and give something of themselves.

SNOWMOBILE RALLY

For those who live in the colder climates and have a lot of snow on the ground, this event is a natural. Make sure that all safety precautions are taken, like helmets, proper clothing, keeping the snowmobiles on a safe course, etc. If a race of some sort is to be run, then it would be best to have the snowmobiles leave at two-minute intervals so that the course does not get crowded or collisions occur. Snowmobiles would race against the clock rather than against each other.

SUPERLATIVES

Have your youth group vote on some "Most Likely to . . ." awards at the end of each school year or at summer camp, etc., only make them really ridiculous. You can have an awards ceremony and perhaps honor a "king" and "queen"—people who got the most nominations. They can get the "royal" treatment, be brought in on a presidential limo (wheelbarrow), and so on. Make up your own categories, but here are a few suggestions:

1. Most likely to burst out laughing at his/her wedding.
2. Most likely to have a complete set of C.S. Lewis books by the toilet in the bathroom.
3. Most likely to move his/her lips to fake singing during church.
4. Most likely to name his/her child something like Elvis, Festus, or Elrod.
5. Most likely to cry when he/she gets an ''A-'' on a test.
6. Most likely to talk in his/her sleep in church.
7. Most likely to feed his/her children granola bars for breakfast.
8. Most likely to have his/her driver's license revoked.
9. Most likely to go through life missing the point of most jokes.
10. Most likely to use the ''we had a flat tire'' excuse on his/her parents.

TRANSGENERATIONAL BASKETBALL

Here's a great way to get your whole church involved in a recreation activity that allows for minimum competition and maximum fellowship. Set up a mixed intramural tournament involving men, women, and youth all on the same team. Each team would consist of two men (adult, college, or high school), one woman (adult, college, or high school), one junior-high girl, and one junior-high boy.

Use regular basketball rules with these restrictions:

1. No fast break on offense
2. No full court pressure on defense
3. Everyone on the team gets to play

The more teams you have the greater your fellowship will be. Plan a round-robin tournament and the last night have refreshments provided for everyone.

WINTER OLYMPICS

If you happen to be fortunate (or unfortunate) enough to live in an area where it snows, ''Winter Olympics'' is a great event that can involve everyone. The games listed below are best played on warmer days when the snow is starting to melt and the sun is shining. A large area such as a football field or park would be ideal.

1. *Three-Man Ski Race:* Using a pair of custom-made three-man skis (see instructions below), have teams of three race a specified distance. Teams can race against the clock, each other, or relay-style.

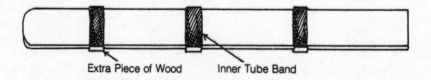

Extra Piece of Wood   Inner Tube Band

Three-man skis are made out of one-inch-thick, 6-foot-by-6-inch boards. With the front end rounded, use three bands of inner tube—bicycle inner tubes work great—for the footholds. Secure the bands to the side of the ski with an extra piece of wood to prevent the rubber from tearing at the nail. Make sure you have the bands tight enough across the ski so that a person's foot can get in with boots. Be sure to bring along an extra band or two and a hammer and nails.

2. *Stilt Relay:* Each team member races on stilts as far as he/she can for thirty seconds. The next team member takes over from that point. Falling forward is not counted in the distance.

3. *Sled Spring:* One person (usually the smallest) sits on a sled, while the rest of the team pulls him/her with a twenty-foot rope. The race course can be straight, up and back, or obstacle.

4. *Snow Mountain:* Teams compete to make the highest mountain of snow. Five minutes is plenty of time.

5. *Snowball Throw:* Kids throw snowballs for distance (have sponsors stand just outside of range for incentive) and accuracy (through tire or other object).

6. *Snow Creation:* Have each team build a figure out of snow to be judged for its artistic quality.

7. *Snowmobile Slalom:* Team members are pulled behind a snowmobile on a giant inner tube and try to grab flags stuck in the snow without falling off tube. Be sure to keep the speed down.

The key to a successful "Winter Olympics" is to be well prepared and keep the event short and lively. Ice-cold young people don't cooperate very well. Afterwards be sure to have a nice warm building where the kids can warm up with hot chocolate and a warm fire.

Service Projects

Service Projects

BREAD-BAKING BASH

Have the kids in your youth group gather all the ingredients they need to bake lots of bread—both loaves and rolls. Then have a day of bread baking (a Saturday works best), first preparing the dough and getting it into pans, then letting it rise. While it's rising, the kids can play some games and just have a good time until the bread is baked.

When the bread is finished, prepare some soup and have a lunch featuring hot soup and freshly baked bread. (You might have everyone bring a can of soup—any kind—and mix it all together.) After lunch, wrap the remaining loaves (there should be more than the kids eat) and visit the homes of some elderly people in the church. Spend a short time visiting with them and leave them with a homemade loaf of bread, along with a note of appreciation, like "Thanks for being a part of our church family". They'll love it, and it helps to build relationships between the young and the old. You could conclude the day with a discussion of what happened while visiting the elderly and perhaps a Bible lesson relating to "bread".

CARE CHORES

Fill offering baskets (or something similar) with "care chores"—slips of paper on which is written a chore that needs to be performed during the coming week. For example:

1. _____ are members of the church. Could you give them a call?
2. _____ has recently undergone surgery. Could you help him?
3. _____ are not members of the church but lost their home in a fire. Could you help them?

These chores are then passed around and selected by members of the group for action. Phone numbers and addresses should also be included, and the people should be reminded that they should not take a chore unless they plan to accomplish it during that week.

CHRISTMAS MISSIONARY DINNER

Have your youth group become better acquainted with the missionary or missionaries that your church supports. The group can get to know the missionaries they have chosen by corresponding with them and also by reading their newsletters they send from the field.

Then begin making plans for a "Missionary Dinner" sometime in November or early December. There should be Christmas decorations and pictures or letters from the missionaries posted so that people can see them. The youth group can cook and serve the meal, which could include some dishes from the country where the missionaries are serving.

Adults of the church are invited to the dinner; and, following a talent show by the youth and a presentation of the work being done by the missionaries, the people are asked to give a free-will offering. The offering can then be sent to the missionaries as a "Christmas Bonus," which they would not ordinarily receive. It is a good idea to hold this event as early as possible (even early November) if it takes a long time to send the money to them so that it arrives before Christmas.

CLOTHES SEARCH

This service project idea can be done by individuals or in small groups. Give the kids a list of clothes needed by an organization you are familiar with (contact this group ahead of time to find out what items they most need and adjust points accordingly). The kids or groups then have two hours to accumulate as many points as possible. They must start at their own house and go from there. Below is a typical list. Revise this as necessary to fit your situation.

1. Pants (jeans, if possible)—25 points for pants; 50 points for jeans
2. Dresses—70 points per dress
3. Coats—small size 150 points; large size—100 points
4. Shirts—20 points
5. Sweaters—40 points
6. Underwear—50 points
7. Cloth diapers—200 points
8. Shoes—175 points
9. Pajamas—15 points
10. Infant clothing—250 points

You can also set up "Bonus Houses," These are homes where the people have collected some clothes already. Each person or group is given a clue sheet. The first person or group to decipher the clues and get to the "bonus houses" get the clothes at that home. Note: The group that originally did this activity stipulated that after the kids went to their own homes, they have to call a neighbor first, tell them what they were doing before they went to the neighbor's house.

DO-IT-YOURSELF CHRISTMAS CARDS

Why not have your group make their own Christmas cards this year? Use a simple block-printing technique or a collage on construction paper. Or if your group is really talented, you could get into silk screening. Here are some ways to make good use of these cards.

1. If you can make enough, package them in bundles of five or ten and sell them to members of your congregation as a fund-raiser to buy presents for needy children.
2. Ask your pastor for a list of the shut-ins in your congregation and assign each young person one or two names to send a card to.
3. Send cards to every patient in a nearby nursing home or the pediatric ward of your local hospital.

EASTER CAROLING

Everyone goes caroling at Christmas, so why not at Easter as well? Decide where you will be going and be sure to inform ahead of time shut-ins or institutions to whom you plan to sing. Meet an hour or so early to make sure that everyone knows the songs you will be singing. You might invite the pastor to come and administer communion to the shut-ins and others. Another good idea is to have a group of older folk bring flowers to give to those you sing to.

Be creative with the songs. Vary the approach—use solos, quartets, harmony, unison, and narration. Use familiar songs so that those being sung to can join in. If you carol all afternoon, you may want to have a party or supper or a food-and-fellowship get-together afterwards.

OFFICIAL PHOTOGRAPHER

If you have a young person in your group who is handicapped and is unable to participate in some of the more active games, get him/her an instant camera. Teach him how to use it properly and then make him the "Official Youth Group Photographer."

Whenever the youth group gets together, he takes pictures, and the kids always gather around him to see how the pictures turn out. This provides an otherwise neglected young person a good opportunity to get lots of attention and to really feel needed and appreciated. The photos can be hung up on the youth group bulletin board. Be sure to use an instant camera—for obvious reasons. Otherwise the results are not the same.

WINDSHIELD WITNESSING

Find a parking lot with a lot of cars in it and supply the youth group with window cleaning materials (soap, rags, squeegees, etc.). The kids move up and down rows in pairs and clean dirty windshields on cars, leaving a note similar to this:

> YOUR WINDOWS HAVE BEEN CLEANED
> WITH LOVE BY THE YOUTH OF
> MAIN ST. COMMUNITY CHURCH. WE JUST
> WANTED TO DO SOMETHING NICE FOR
> PEOPLE TODAY TO DEMONSTRATE
> THE LOVE OF CHRIST, AND WE HOPE
> THAT'S OK WITH YOU. WE ALSO HOPE
> YOU'LL SEE YOUR WAY CLEAR TO
> ATTEND THE CHURCH OF YOUR CHOICE
> NEXT SUNDAY.

Some people may want to make a donation to the youth group, but make sure the kids do this strictly for free. People will really appreciate it, especially nowadays when it is hard to find a service station that will clean your windows.

THE YOUNG AND THE WISE BANQUET

This event is both a service project and a fun activity for church youth groups. The young people plan a banquet, complete with a program, and invite the senior citizens of the church to come as their guests. The youth either pay for the food (catered), bring it potluck-style, or prepare it themselves. However, it is usually best that the kids not spend too much with meal preparation, as they need to have time to spend with their invited guests. Each young person is assigned certain senior citizens to pick up, take home, and sit with during the banquet. Invitations are sent to the senior citizens along with R.S.V.P. forms that they can send back. Be sure to plan a menu that senior citizens can eat, keep the program brief and lively, make plans several weeks in advance, and promote it well; you'll be assured of a successful evening. One church has done this two years in a row with more than 175 senior citizens attending each year.

Fund-raisers

Fund-raisers

FUN RUN

Running is something that people do for fun and for good health these days, instead of running just to get somewhere fast. People even pay money (lots of it) to run. They buy running shoes, shorts, sweat bands, magazines on running, and often even pay to enter races. So, why not capitalize on this and have a "Fun Run"?

All you have to do is find a course or track and a suitable day, and then get the word out. The race should be short for kids, longer for adults, and everyone who enters can be given a special "Fun Run" T-shirt, which you can have made up ahead of time. Each entrant pays four or five dollars to enter; and depending on the cost of the shirts and trophies for the winners, it is possible to come out ahead on the venture and have a good time, too. Do it in cooperation with the YMCA or local athletic clubs and you might be surprised by the response you get.

READ-A-THON

This has also been called a "Bible-a-thon," but the "Read-a-thon" is a little more flexible. The idea is simply to choose a weekend or other period of time and read (from the Bible or from other Christian literature) continuously for as long as possible. One group did this beginning on a Friday afternoon. They read from the Bible nonstop until the Sunday morning service. One person would read while everyone else in the group sat in the audience and followed along. The readers would switch off during the entire time, each reading for as long as he/she could. The group was able to read all of Genesis, Exodus, Joshua, Judges, Ruth, 1 and 2 Samuel, 1 and 2 Kings, Job, Psalms, Proverbs, Eccleciastes, Song of Solomon, Isaiah, Jonah, Daniel, Matthew, John, Acts, Romans, 1 and 2 Corinthians, Galatians, Ephesians, Philippians, 1 and 2 John, and Revelation.

149

Each young person obtains sponsors for himself, who pledge a certain amount for each hour of continuous reading. It turns out to be a pretty good sum if they really work at it. For example, thirty kids getting about $5.00 per hour in pledges can raise around $3,600 for only one twenty-four-hour day. But what makes this fund-raiser really different is that you can also arrange to have someone record the entire Read-a-thon on cassette tapes. These tapes can then be used to provide the Bible or other literature to elderly people who find it difficult to read or to the blind. When it is recorded, it also insures that the kids will read carefully.

The advantage to reading something other than Scripture is that there is always the danger that someone might get so sick of reading the Bible after this ordeal that he never picks it up again. So you might consider reading C. S. Lewis, Tolkien, or any other good literature that kids can learn from as well as enjoy. But the Bible can be used as long as the experience is a good one and not forced on anyone. Be sure to give kids periodic breaks (five minutes per hour) to eat, stretch, go to the bathroom, and so on. Also require them to get plenty of rest before the event, and allow anyone to quit whenever he/she wants to.

SPLASH AND SPLIT

For this activity the youth group travels up and down streets washing windows on houses as a service project. Of course, the people who live in each house should be asked first, but it's rare for anyone to turn it down. The group should do it for free, just as a way to show the community that Christian love is more than just words.

This can also be done as a fund-raiser if donations are accepted for the window washing. Take whatever people feel that they can pay, or charge a modest fee, like five dollars or less per house. Most people hate to wash their own windows. With a group of give or ten kids, the job can be done rather quickly.

TRASH-A-THON

One problem with most "-athons" is that they accomplish little or nothing other than raising money. The trash-a-thon, however, strikes a blow for a better environment as it makes the bucks. What happens is that the kids—instead of sitting in a rocking chair, taking a hike, or riding a bike—pick up litter. They get people to sponsor them for a certain amount of money for each large trash bag full of litter they pick up. Your city or county health or pollution department may be able to help you find the area most in need. If the area is littered enough, each kid can easily pick up fifteen to twenty bags in about five hours. This project appeals to their sponsors in that they are helping clean up your town as well as helping your kids. You may be able to talk a local merchant into providing a couple of prizes, e.g., one prize for the person with the most sponsors and another for the one who picks up the most trash.

The Family

The Family

PARENT YOUTH NIGHTS

Here's a six-week program for parents and teenagers that works well in place of your mid-week age group meetings. Make sure that you let both the parents and youth know that the series is not loaded in anyone's favor.

FIRST WEEK: "Parents Party"

Have just a plain old-fashioned party with games, singing, and refreshments planned and run by the kids. After the party have the group meet together to discuss the upcoming series of meetings.

SECOND WEEK: "Family Bridge"

Here is a great idea that involves both parents and kids in a cooperative activity. The group should be divided into teams of parents and kids (families should be mixed so that the parents are on a different team than their kids).

The task is to construct a single cardboard "bridge" between two "cliffs" separated by a ten-foot "river." The bands of the "river" should be marked by placing masking tape on the floor beyond the edges of the tables.

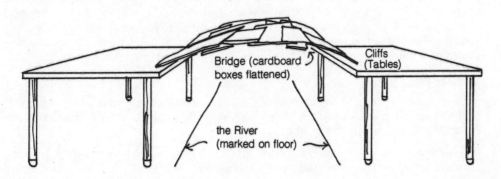

Bridge (cardboard boxes flattened)

Cliffs (Tables)

the River (marked on floor)

Each team of builders constructs their part of the "bridge" using cardboard boxes (broken flat), string, and masking tape. The teams cannot speak directly to the other side nor can they enter the ten-foot-wide "river" between the "cliffs." But each team can appoint a Negotiator (with arm band) and a Job Foreman (complete with hard hat) who meet in the middle of the "river" to exchange strategy every ten minutes or more if needed, but only for one minute each time.

The Job Foreman coordinates his/her team efforts to construct their portion of the "bridge."

The difficulty comes when both sides have to be joined in the middle. Since none of the builders can work in the "river" the task gets rather complicated. Remember, neither team can communicate directly with each other. The "bridge" cannot touch the floor nor the ceiling but must be suspended between the two "cliffs."

The teams have forty-five minutes to construct the "bridge." When construction is over, the "bridge" is tested by placing a heavy weight in the middle of the "bridge" (like a giant Bible).

If it stands the test, you can have a celebration ceremony and follow with a discussion.

THIRD WEEK: "Getting to Know You"

Develop a series of question-and-answer games to see if the parents and young people know as much about themselves as they think they do. Utilize the Serendipity Series by Lyman Coleman that is directed toward families.

FOURTH WEEK: "Family at Play"

A discussion of what families do together. Have the families share their traditions, special days, events, camping trips, family nights, and games that they enjoy as a family.

FIFTH WEEK: "Family at Worship"

Be careful with this one. Some families may not do much together in this area, so be sure to begin with lots of suggestions for what families *can* do. It would also be good to discuss why it is so difficult for families to get together for anything, especially spiritual matters. You might then ask if there are any families doing anything in the area of family devotions, reading, prayer, etc., and have them share.

SIXTH WEEK: "Families Alive"

The purpose of this game is to symbolically demonstrate the importance of cooperation among families. "Families Alive" is primarily a game but does require cooperation in order for each family to enjoy.

The game is designed to be completed quickly (twenty to thirty minutes) but is not a race. Each family is to complete ten symbolic activities which are performed at ten separate stations. Each station should be twenty to fifty feet apart and should be identified to prevent confusion. "Restoring Human Dignity" must be done first and "Living Spring" done last. All others can be done at random when the station is vacant. Each family checks off the activities as completed.

To begin the game a flare is lit representing the time remaining before the world ends. As long as a flare is lit, the game proceeds, so have several flares on hand to relight as others burn out. When the flares are out, the game is over.

Give the following sheet to each family:

_____ 1. *Restore Human Dignity* — Tie a balloon on each other's waist. (Human Dignity must be maintained throughout the game.) If a balloon breaks you must go back to the Human Dignity Station to obtain another.

_____ 2. *Feed the Hungry* — Feed each other crackers.

_____ 3. *Free the Captives* — Blindfold all members but one, for he will lead you to the next station. Remove the blindfolds and return them to the station *before* doing the next activity.

_____ 4. *Rebuild the Nations* — Build a tower by stacking the empty milk cartons. They must remain stacked for 15 seconds.

_____ 5. *Clean Up the Environment* — Line up in a straight line. Take a sheet of paper, crumple it up, and pass it down the line to the last person, who drops it into the trash can.

_____ 6. *Heal the Sick* — Put a "band-aid" on each other. Each person does all the others in the family, so you will have one from all members. Leave the tape on until the game is over.

_____ 7. *Clothe the Naked* — Put on a coat and hat and give it to the next member until all have had a turn.

_____ 8. *Welcome Strangers* — Stop another family and greet each of their members, shaking hands and inviting them to visit you again.

_____ 9. *Preach the Word* — Select a family member to read aloud Matthew 25:31–46.

_____10. *Living Spring* — After you have completed all of the above activities, take a cup and fill it full of water from the Living Spring and each member take a sip of water from it. Refill the cup and pour it into the second water container. Wait nearby once you have finished.

Once all families have completed all activities, pour the bucket of water over the flare to extinguish it. Then have the families join together for a discussion of the evening's activities.